More Than a Race

More Than a Race

*Four 70-year-old Cyclists ride the
Race Across America*

Don Metz

Mill City Press, Minneapolis

Mill City Press, Inc.
212 3rd Avenue North, Suite 290
Minneapolis, MN 55401
612.455.2294
www.millcitypublishing.com

ISBN-13: 978-1-62652-196-4
LCCN: 2013909997

Cover Design by Karen Scheerer
Typeset by Mary Kristin Ross

Printed in the United States of America

Prologue
Three weeks before the 2012 RAAM

I've come to the Alewife train station on this beautiful May afternoon to pick up my friend Paula. She's taking the T from Massachusetts General Hospital, where she's soldiering through a series of chemo and radiation treatments. Paula is unusually pretty, petite and amazingly robust despite her recent ordeal. We come from the same little town in New Hampshire where we both became hooked on racing bicycles to the brink of hypoxia. Both she and I have stood on victors' podia at Mount Washington, Whiteface Mountain and the Appalachian Gap, among others. The bicycles we own -- and serious cyclists are never satisfied with just one (or four) -- are lightweight, absurdly high-tech, and cost about the same as 12 months of intensive psychotherapy.

The Alewife parking garage is vast and dark, and I'm naturally drawn to the brightness at the western edge, where two long, parallel rows of commuters' bicycles are locked to steel stanchions. Fendered, basketed, fat-tired and rusted, these work horses are exactly what I would favor if I were commuting. Some have been vandalized, wheels and seats missing, but most appear ready to ride. I'm encouraged to see the commuter cycling culture has become so popular.

Picture me, then, a tall, skinny guy, north of 70, clean shaven, no visible prison tattoos, walking slowly by these rows of commuter bikes. I'm wearing ridiculous blue Crocs with no socks, khaki shorts and a T-shirt. If you were to profile "harmless", I'd be your poster boy.

The transit policeman cruising by thinks differently.

He leans across the passenger seat of his SUV and says, "Can I help you?"

"I'm waiting for a friend," I say.

"You're looking at the bikes," he says. "Any particular reason?"

"Just curious," I say. When I continue eyeing the bikes, he turns off his engine and hastens over to me. He's large and purposefully intimidating. My voice betrays an edge of unease when I offer, "I'm a cyclist." But I can see he's not satisfied with my answer, so I add, "I ride a lot."

"Sure you do." He opens a note pad and jots something down. "I ride a lot, too," he says, suggesting we're both bluffing. "But you shouldn't be looking at these bikes, okay?" He cradles my elbow and steers me away from the row of what he imagines to be irresistible temptations. "You ever been arrested?"

"No, Sir," I say, surrendering to a rise of impatience. *Could it really be illegal to look at parked bikes?* I've been riding over 300 miles a week in preparation for the 3,000-mile Race Across America, which begins in three weeks. I don't have time to be arrested -- or, for that matter -- to be unfairly interrogated. Training has pre-occupied my life for the last 8 months, and the hoped-for rewards are, as yet, uncertain. My passion and respect for cycling makes the idea of stealing someone's old commuter bike absurd. I am waiting for a friend who is fighting for her life, and although it may be this policeman's job to protect these bikes, just as I would want him to protect mine if I were a commuter, his suspicions are misplaced and -- insulting.

He says, "Let me see your driver's license."

The last thing I need now is to act on the exasperation I'm feeling, get hauled off to a precinct station and leave no one to greet Paula. I want to get this over with, so I do as I'm told. He examines my license, jabs at his cell phone and makes two or three futile calls to assess my criminality. I hear him repeat my name several times. My naive hope is that the people he's calling are not interested in his bogus problem, or maybe they're not answering because *they* know I'm innocent. While he's dialing, I decide to look ever more covetously at the bikes he thinks I'm about to steal. I want to justify my right to do so, or maybe just to piss him off. When it appears he's satisfied that I'm not on the 10 most-wanted list, he abruptly hands back my license and orders me over to the waiting area, 50 yards away. As I start walking, I can't resist the urge to assert myself one last time, and I ask, "So, what kind of bike do you ride?"

He has the badge and the uniform, and his bike-thief theory is professionally embarrassing, so I understand why he plays his trump card. "One more word out of you" he says, "and I will have you removed from these premises." He is not having a good day. "Get over there *now!*"

"Maybe Paula and I can go for a ride today," I say to myself, walking as slowly as I dare towards a group of onlookers staring at us from the waiting area benches. *"Maybe we'll go up by the golf course, nice easy pace in the sun, take some lunch and enjoy the view."* When I see her striding up the steps looking as strong and beautiful as ever, I snap back to the realization that, compared to life's serious challenges, this little episode was nothing.

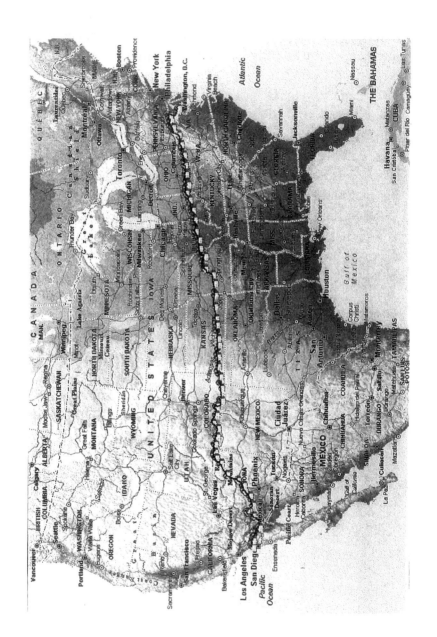

Beginnings

The Race Across America held its first event in 1982 with a field of four soloists who rode from the Santa Monica Pier in Los Angeles to the Empire State Building in New York City. The race attracted a growing number of riders in the following years, and team divisions were added in 1992, by which time the "RAAM" had emerged as an international event. Enthusiasm for cycling in America has grown exponentially ever since, and in no small measure, its popularity is linked to this epic event.

Compared to the Tour de France, a stage-per-day race which averages 2,000 miles in length and takes 23 days to complete, the RAAM is a non-stop, start-to-finish contest averaging 3,000 miles, and is completed within 5 or 10 days, depending upon the team classification. RAAM competitors have no peloton to draft behind, no restaurant meals, no soft beds, and the clock never stops until the finish line is crossed. The RAAM includes 2, 4, and 8-person teams, as well as the super-human soloists who ride for up to 22 hours per day. There are few enterprises on earth that demand such extremes of stamina as these soloists endure. In 1986, Pete Penseyres rode across the country in 8 days, 9 hours and 47 minutes. His average speed was 15.40 mph, establishing the men's solo record, which stands today. Not a race for men only, about 15% of RAAM's competitors are women. Seana Hogan set the women's RAAM solo record in 1995 at 9 days, 4 hours and 2 minutes, at an average speed of 13.22 mph.

The fastest RAAM *team* record was set by the 2012, 8-man Team ViaSat, USA, which pedaled from Oceanside, CA to Annapolis, MD in 5 days, 5 hours and 5 minutes at an average speed of 23.93 mph ! Comparing Team ViaSat's performance with an automobile traveling at 60 mph for 8 hours a day would bring the driver to Annapolis in 6 days and 6 hours -- 25 hours *slower* than the record-setting cyclists.

Of course, the RAAM is not for everyone. While an inactive, 200-lb. American male might consume 3,000 calories a day and continue to gain unwanted weight, that same day might see a 150-lb. RAAM racer consume 7,000 calories and *lose* weight. Despite the hardships, some racers find the RAAM experience addictive. Recidivist Rob Kash has completed the race 19 times, Seana Hogan 6 times. If these numbers reflect gender differences, one might conclude that men are more durable than women -- or, women are 3 times more intelligent.

Bicycle racing in the USA has yet to equal its status abroad, which perhaps explains why 36 of the 45 soloists entered in 2012 were natives of 19 other countries, including China, India, Slovenia, the Russian Federation, Taiwan and New Zealand. The 2012 RAAM drew teams from 9 countries, including Brazil, the UK, Angola and Australia. About 40 % of the racers are from outside the U.S.

RAAM events raise more than $2 million annually for a wide range of charitable causes. The RAAM is operated by a privately-owned, for-profit organization with an outstanding safety record and a tradition of careful preparation. Crew chief seminars are mandatory, as are qualifying events for soloists. Prior to each year's event, RAAM's Boulder, CO headquarters publishes an updated, comprehensive route book with GPS compatibility. Every racer's support crew is utterly dependent upon this race Bible for the precise mileage at every turn, including occasional chilling cautions, such as: *"Watch for elk crossing the road at night."*

The most persistent, interesting question about the RAAM is, *why?* Why do ostensibly competent, sane individuals choose to risk so much danger and endure so much discomfort? Is extreme suffering simply masochistic, or can it be understood as a healthy obsession leading to revelations nowhere else to be found ? How does the RAAM experience compare with sailing solo around the world or climbing Mt. Everest? Are the motives leading to these extreme adventures to be interpreted as the narcissistic indulgences of needy egos, or is there a common, redeeming quality among them?

The United4Health Race Team

Dave Burnett, "Dur" Higgins, Don Metz and Michael Patterson

MORE THAN A RACE is an account of a 4-man, septuagenarian team's experience in the Race Across America, the ultimate cycling adventure. The lifelong journeys that brought each member of the team to the starting line, and what compelled them to overcome the hardships that followed, is told from many points of view, but behind each of those stories is a common denominator: From the beginning, Michael Patterson was the instigator, tireless organizer and unassuming captain of our 2012 RAAM team. It was he who long ago decided the RAAM was a worthy goal for his 8th decade. It was he who selected his team mates, found an enthusiastic sponsor in UnitedHealthcare, hosted a late winter training camp in Tucson, and signed up Dave Eldridge, the best crew chief in RAAM history. Without Michael's tireless, modest and judicious leadership, there would never have been a Team United4Health in the Race Across America.

Elena Patterson

"In 1995, at a Morgan ski event in Vail, Michael ran into Jim Kennedy, who had just done the RAAM. The more Jim talked about it, the more Michael was intrigued. A few months later, we had dinner with some friends to discuss the possibilities of doing this crazy event. For them, it was a lark, but for Michael it kept percolating on the back burner. After he started racing seriously, the RAAM was something I started to hear about often. With retirement in

sight, he really needed something to take the place of his demanding career.

Michael had no idea of what this race would entail, but he began making plans. At the beginning of 2010 he called his college roommate and tried to persuade him to give up drinking, start training and consider being a member of the team. His roommate knew right away that the RAAM was not for him. Michael also tried to get another old friend to be crew chief. They flew to Raleigh-Durham for a RAAM crew chief seminar, but this friend also thought the RAAM was more than he could tackle. Michael, meanwhile, was not to be deterred.

During the spring of 2010, I heard more and more about the RAAM. Michael talked to friends about getting a sponsor, although he was willing to fund the operation himself, so I knew he was serious. A clear choice for sponsors would be a product or an organization having to do with health. Mary Mundinger, Dean of Columbia's School of Nursing, is a good friend of Michael's, and she was on the Board of UnitedHealthcare. Mary has always been interested in Michael's exploits, and it was her introduction to Reed Tuckson that started the talks with UnitedHealthcare, which ultimately became the team's generous sponsor.

It was not until October of 2010 at the Huntsman Senior Games in Utah that I realized this was definitely going to happen. After Michael won the criterium, Durward Higgins and his wife Earline came to congratulate Michael, at which point I learned he'd already invited Dur to be a member of a RAAM team. Dur was interested, but Earline asked many questions, and I could tell she was intrigued. As we left, Michael told them he would send them a film on the RAAM.

Michael soon had his first teammate. Now to find the 2 others. Not long after our return from Utah, we got a *call from Dave Burnett, who had heard that Michael was on the Board of USA Cycling, and wanted to come speak to him. As is Michael's way, he invited Dave for a ride and lunch with 2 other cyclists. (This may have been the beginning of Dave's infatuation with my chef salad.) As we were sitting there at lunch, the subject of the RAAM came up, and Dave immediately invited himself to be a member of the team. No one at that moment realized that Dave, at 68, was not old enough to qualify for the 70+ age category. But since the age category was based on average age, Dave insisted it would be no problem to find a 4th cyclist 72 years old. Dave immediately thought of his friend John, and we invited him and his wife to come to dinner with the Burnetts and us. I prepared a delicious dinner to help sell them on the race, but the minute they came in, I felt it was a no go. Not long into the evening John's wife came into the kitchen and told me there was no way her husband was doing the race. I relayed the message after they left, and at first, I don't think Dave or Michael thought she was serious. A few days later, Michael received a call saying John would not be able to participate. Now the question was, who?*

During those days, the RAAM was almost the only thing Michael could talk about, and maybe that was a good thing as he was out riding with his friend Ken Hochman and mentioned his dilemma of finding a 72 year-old cyclist. Ken had a cycling friend he had met in New Hampshire while visiting his son at Dartmouth, and suggested Michael call Don Metz. Don is a Yale graduate, architect, author, but most importantly, a hill climber and racer, and even more importantly, he was intrigued with the notion of the RAAM and soon agreed to join the team. It was during this time that we also met Phil Southerland, who was a founder of Team Type 1 which had set a RAAM record. One thing led to another, and Phil suggested Michael contact Dave Eldridge to see if he was available to be the crew chief. Little by little, everything was coming together.

In November of 2011, we had a visit in New York from Dave Eldridge and his indispensible co-chief, Karen Scheerer. They had just finished supporting the Run Across America with Team Type 1, and now, I think they wanted see Michael in person and make sure he was all there. We had a delightful evening together. Dave and Karen were definitely responsible people. They had done the RAAM numerous times, and I felt entirely comfortable with Michael putting himself and his team in their hands.

Early in 2012, we rented a house in Tucson where we spent 2 glorious months. It was there that most of the remaining groundwork took place, including a 2-week training session with all 4 of the racers, plus a weekend visit from Dave Eldridge, who wanted to make sure that these men were serious and not just a bunch of geezers out for a good time. I awaited the arrival of the team with trepidation. They were staying at another rented house, but would be having dinner with us every night. I luckily found a young woman chef, who delivered our evening meals, all delicious. The team was following coach Aidan Charles' plan, doing however-many kilojoules during their daily rides. On the days they came back for lunch, I felt we hardly ever had enough of Dave Burnett's favorite salad, so we supplemented it with ice cream, which they all loved. They had wonderful training sessions, which included some local riders, mostly John Markley, who had volunteered to be a member of the RAAM crew in June."

Aside from a weekend's ride the previous autumn, the 2 weeks in Tucson would be the first and only time that Michael, Dave, Dur and I would ever spend so much time together before, or during, the RAAM. As competitive, alpha males, it took a few hours to sort ourselves out, but the lack of chest bumping was encouraging. We were in sunny Tucson, after all, blessed to be doing what we loved to do, and life was refreshingly simple: ride, eat, sleep; get up and do it all over again. Among our many routes were Mt. Lemmon (twice), Gates Pass, Kitt Peak, Coronado State Park, up north to Saddlebrook,, and down south to a loop from Sonoita to Parker Lake and back -- about 330 miles each week.

Creating relationships around a single, engaging activity reveals a lot about who we are within that paradigm, but provides only clues as to who we may be in other circumstances. Since our goal was reductively straightforward: break the RAAM record, we were focused on who we could be as a racing team, *period*. We rarely discussed other aspects of our lives -- family, work, politics, existential hopes and fears -- but what I learned about my teammates gave me confidence that we had the stuff to ride ourselves deep into the RAAM record books.

About our respective racing abilities, let me just say that they seemed remarkably strong, varied in style, but impressive all around. Given the level of conspicuous talent, I was otherwise convinced that our success would ultimately hinge on "character" rather than a few percentage points' more conditioning, and character was what emerged in Tucson. Let me start with Dur Higgins, who arrived with his bicycle in a homemade suitcase; 1/8th-inch plywood with hardwood corners. Aside from being 30% smaller and 50% lighter than the typical clumsy, commercial models, Dur's creation included ingenious methods of dismantling and packing the bike. A career engineer and unapologetic "weight weenie", Dur's attention to his custom suitcase became for me a fitting correlative for his perfectionist, scientific approach to all aspects of cycling. The Swiss watch precision that went into the design of that bike box persuaded me, a career architect attuned to complex efficiencies, that Dur would coax every fraction of advantage out of any obstacle he might encounter. And, as if to complement his brilliant engineering skills, Dur revealed himself to be an enthusiastic admirer of classic Broadway musicals.

Dave Burnett seemed almost Dur's opposite. Where Dur relied on physics and formulae, Dave relied on physicality and emotion. I saw in Dave a fervor for racing that transcended equipment or conditions: He would race a rusty tricycle through a cornfield if that was the contest of the day. Dave's love of the chase was palpable. For him, a pace line breakaway was irresistible. Where Dur might find an advantage in discarding 100 grams of unnecessary weight, Dave would no doubt find an advantage in pure desire. Where Dur might analyze and cleverly re-invent a solution to a tricky problem, Dave would ride hell-bent through it -- and it seemed likely to me that they both might achieve the same results. Dave, I thought, would bring passion to the two-wheeled Passion Play we'd soon play out on the roads across America. Dave was the one among us we could trust to volunteer for the hero's role whenever it might be offered.

Michael Patterson's steady competence and focused energy gave the team its gravitational center. At once gracious and reserved, it was rare that Michael spoke ill of anyone. Indifferent to small talk, when he voiced an opinion, it was diplomatically balanced and levelheaded. I sensed he often knew much more than he revealed, but that he felt no need to add what might be considered contentious or superfluous details. When Michael offered a compliment, he meant it. His past years of training with coach Aidan Charles, plus his dedicated adherence to weight work, flexibility and sports massage, were indicative of his immense resolve to exceed -- extra efforts which, in their particulars, were unique among us. I found Michael's calm and steady manner always reassuring, if at times, enigmatic. Matching his apparent conservatism to his preferred iTunes play list -- Bob Seeger, The Rolling Stones and Jefferson Airplane -- was for me a fascinating insight into an intriguing, complex personality.

Elena Patterson

"Who would have thought that four 70-year-olds would care so much about the team kit? Bib-shorts vs. regular shorts, skin suits, colors, how many of each -- the discussion of, 'Do we need a jacket or not?' sounded like a bunch of teenagers deciding what to wear to the prom. Dave Eldridge finally said they needed the jacket, and I don't know about the rest of the team, but Michael wears his all the time.

The rest of 2012 was all about training for the RAAM. The team was determined to avoid the risk of injury, so there was none of the usual, early-season racing -- not that there were no injuries, but at least there were none due to racing. Instead, they went through weeks and weeks of grueling workouts, full of enthusiasm mixed with a little bit of angst and a lot of fatigue. I can honestly say those last few months were awful. Michael would go out on weekends for 6 to 8 hours to practice the 20 minutes on, 20 minutes off race simulation. He became a legendary figure in our commuter parking lot.

As the race-date approached and everything was settled, Michael heard that *his friend, Reed Tuckson, had written a book called, 'The Doctor in the Mirror', so he down-loaded it and came to a passage which began, 'Let me give you an example of a gentleman I recently met who is an absolute inspiration. I'm going to call him 'The Sultan of Cycling'. The Sultan and three other 70-somethings will each take turns cycling. . . from California all the way to the East Coast.'"*

Dave Eldridge, crew chief

"I'm 60 years old and was raised in Ohio in a family of nine children-- five brothers and three sisters. I graduated college with a BS in Education in 1978, and for 25years had a professional career in mortgage banking. I've been married to Joyce for 38 years and we have two sons and four grandchildren. Currently, I'm a semi-retired, professional consultant. Cycling experience: None. (I don't ride !)

My son Joe is the co-founder of Team Type 1. TT1 was created as a diabetes awareness group with an emphasis on cycling as the platform to deliver the team's message of inspiration to individuals and families with diabetes. My first RAAM was in support of a team of all diabetic cyclists. I served as a crew member in 2006 and 2007, then I served as crew chief for TT1 in 2008, 2009, and 2010. During that five-year period, TT1 finished first or second each year in the eight-man category.

When Michael Patterson called in 2011 and asked me to be crew chief for his team of 70- year-olds, I didn't know what to think. He sounded solid, but did he and his teammates really know what this race demanded of its riders? Was he a weekend warrior type who goes out on Saturdays, rides 50 miles, and calls it quits for the week? I said I'd call back, and then spent some time researching him and his teammates. It turned out these guys were the accomplished racers he said they were, but I still worried about their age and their ambition. They wanted to beat the record set in 2004 by a team of well-known racers. Fair enough, but could they? I didn't want to spend a lot of time and energy with a team that would fall apart, or make just a mediocre showing.

A few more calls and emails led me to believe this might work, and I signed on. In November of 2011, I finally met Michael at his home in NYC, and was further convinced this was the right decision for me. In the next few weeks, I called in previous RAAM crew members and assembled a majority of tested veterans as well as some promising new recruits. Next came a number of emails and conference calls where I got a better sense of who these racers were, and how they might do as RAAM competitors. The moment of truth came when I flew to Tucson in March where the team was training for 2 weeks using Michael's house as headquarters. We spent a couple of days together, worked on rider exchange drills and went over shift assignments I'd roughed out before my arrival. Michael's wife Elena fed us some delicious meals, and I got to see how these guys interacted among themselves in a social setting -- no problems with team dynamics that I could see. We discussed and ordered United4Health team kits from Pactimo, kicked around shift-length ideas and a dozen other questions the racers had. I got to see how they handled themselves on their bikes and was once again encouraged. These individuals did not look like any 70-yr-olds I knew. They had the bodies and ambitions of much younger men, and by the time I left Tucson, I was hoping we might break the old record by enough to see it stand for a good, long while. The record we were out to beat was 7 days, 16 hours and 31 minutes, which translated to an average of 16.03 mph. I decided to raise the target to 18 mph -- 7 days even -- which I thought would be at the higher end of probabilities, but still allowed a margin in which we could achieve a new record. From that point on, at the bottom of every one of my emails was the line, "18 mph, 168 hours, No penalties, No injuries, New RAAM record."

DAY ONE
Oceanside, CA to Prescott, AZ
441 miles

It's half-past noon on June 16th, 2012 near the starting line of the Race Across America, *"The toughest bicycle race in the world."* The staging area stretches for hundreds of yards along the Strand at Oceanside, CA. Warm ocean breezes sway the palms as a colorful festival of journalists, vendors, team support crews and loyal well-wishers mingle with 256 hopeful cyclists. Our "United4Health" team is alphabetically destined to be next-to-last to depart, and as we wait through the 1-minute departure intervals, we jockey for position beneath what scarce shade is available, a pedestrian bridge here, a stairway there. These brief escapes from the heat are symbolic at best. The hours we'll soon spend under a merciless sun will bear no comparison to these anxious, idle moments by the sea.

Our team's average age is 70. Staged next to us, as if to emphasize the audacity of our ambition, is Team 26 from Germany; the number refers to the racers' average age. They could be our grandsons, sleek and whippet-thin. But we're not racing against them, or anyone else here today. Instead, we are chasing down a record set by 4 men whose average age was also 70, the Grand PAC Masters -- Bob Kash, Lee Mitchell, Ron Bell and Chris Stauffer. In 2004, they crossed the country in 7 days, 16 hours and 31 minutes. Their average speed was 16.03 mph. We intend to do better.

Along with the scores of men and women racers waiting impatiently in line with us is a fortune in exotic bicycles, some of them worth well over $10,000. These lightweight titanium alloys and hand-crafted, steel and carbon fiber frames bear the marques of the world's finest manufacturers.

There are TT (time trial) bikes, road racing bikes and the odd, lay-back, feet-first recumbent configurations, all sporting an assortment of featherweight wheels and race-proven components. Dressed in bright and bold team kits from all over the world, every cyclist here looks ultra-fit and invincible, and while we are arguably in the best condition of our lives, it's both a comfort and a cautionary omen to know there are 4 racers in this year's RAAM who are older. Two of them, Ron Bell and Chris Stauffer, were on the 70+ team whose 2004 record we are chasing down. This year, they've joined Daniel Telep and Lew Meyer to form the first RAAM team whose average age is 80.

Our impatience gives way to excitement as we're swept at last towards the starting line. By this time tomorrow, we'll begin to truly know the nature of this cycling beast. Our pre-conceived ideas will be tested. Is there any other way to know this race without completing it? While seagulls soar above the white-capped surf, the race director motions us to the starting line and introduces us. The crowd applauds, we ready our bikes and he signals our departure; one pedal stroke, two pedal strokes, we turn our backs to the blue Pacific and move off into an uncertain future.

The journey begins with all 4 of us riding a "parade formation" along the San Luis Rey River Bike Trail, which provides the most direct, traffic-free route away from coastal congestion. According to the rules, we have no choice but to proceed slowly on this narrow path, which is both frustrating and exhilarating; we are finally, finally, *finally* entering into the dream of the legendary RAAM. The sun is shining, temperatures are in the mid-70s, and we have a sweet little tailwind. When I perform my habitual bike check/body scan, a ritual I will repeat a hundred times across the country, I confirm that my bike is shifting smoothly, there are no chafing sounds of misaligned brakes or derailleurs, the tires are fully inflated, my legs feel springy, my arms and back are loose, my breath is barely audible and my butt is settled into a dry and comfortable chamois. All is well with 2,993 miles to go. With so much of the unknown before us, I wonder if the thousands of miles we spent training will be adequate, and if the crew is as competent as it seems to be. RAAM lore emphasizes that the world's best crew can't win the race for unprepared racers, and, conversely, the world's best racers can lose the race due to an unprepared crew. But we are lucky to have a crew chief with 5 successful campaigns to his credit, and since the idea of failure is useless to contemplate, I turn my face to the sun and pedal into the pleasure of the moment.

Eight miles out, we come to the end of the parade lap at Mance Buchanon Park, and it's from here that the RAAM really begins. As planned, our 4-man team will be divided into two, 2-man teams, Michael and Dave comprising one, Dur and I the other. While one pair races a shift of somewhere between 8 and 9 hours, depending on the mileage and the terrain, the other rests. When a shift is over, the in-coming team begins its rest period and the out-going team races the next 8 to 9-hour shift. Racing in relay fashion, one of us will be on the road in alternating, 20 to 25- minute rotations, at all times, night and day, until we reach Annapolis.

Michael and Dave are scheduled to race the first 145 miles, and they are already gone by the time the crew has loaded our bikes onto the rear-mounted racks and hustled Dur and me into an air-conditioned van. Our 15-person support crew is spread out among 5 vehicles. Three of the crew are dedicated to being with the racers at all times in the **racer van,** two at a time while the third takes a rest shift. Another three, also rotating two on, one off, are protecting the racers at all times in the **follow van**, which

THE ARMADA

CREW RV

LEWIS RUNNION
HOWARD CONWAY
JAN SMOLOWITZ
MANNY CASILLAS
2 van crew in rotation

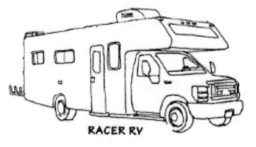

RACER RV

BARNY BRANNEN
MICHAEL SCHOLL
LYDIA BREWSTER
2 racers in rotation

FOLLOW VAN

JOHN MARKLEY
GREG THOMPSON
KEN GUNNELLS

RACER VAN

CHRIS CHAMPION
TAYLOR KEATON
NATE KECK

CREW CHIEF VAN

DAVE ELDRIDGE
KAREN SCHEERER

Stiles Designs

is driven about 50 ft. behind the racer with its warning lights flashing. Another 2 of the crew are the drivers/navigators of the **Racers' RV**, and 2 more share the same duties in the **Crew's RV**, which also carries our masseuse, nutritionist and RN. **The crew chief's van**, carrying crew chief Dave Eldridge and his co-chief, Karen Scheerer, acts as an auxiliary vehicle to take care of all unforeseen issues -- of which we will have our share.

Chris Champion, racer van driver/navigator

"We were on the first rotation, with Dave and Michael on the road, and as we descended into Borego Springs, through Christmas Circle, we were parked up against another team for a transition. The shoulder was wide, and from our vantage point behind the other team, we could see them get their rider ready for their incoming guy. Because our rider was also there, the 'sterile cockpit' wasn't possible: some chit-chat was happening between teams, friendly enough. Their rider came in first, the transition was quick, and the outgoing rider took off -- and turned right -- off course! His team mates hadn't seen the mistake because they were walking the incoming rider back to their van. Decked out in time trial helmet and on a bike with noisy disc wheels, the rider shot down the wrong road, unable to hear us yelling. The other team started saying, 'What are you shouting at?' and we told them: 'Your rider is going the wrong way!' At first they didn't believe us (did they think we were trying to mess with them?), but then they saw him: head down, pedaling fast, headed back to San Diego. Bewildered, they jumped in their van and gave chase. I don't recall seeing them again."

The route Michael and Dave ride from one o'clock in the afternoon until dark takes them across 75 hot miles from sea level up to the 4,200 ft. crest of the Coast Range, then down onto the scorching floor of the Anza Borrego Desert and across the wide, hot Imperial Valley. While Dur and I are dutifully asleep all afternoon in the air-conditioned racers' RV, Michael and Dave are hammering along Rte 78, south of the Salton Sea at 200 ft. below sea level. We are oblivious to their immense efforts as they cross flat stretches of sand-blown desert in treacherous temperatures. This first leg of the RAAM delivers the thrill of racing after months of preparation, but it is not without its dangers. The hot, fast flats, steep inclines and gripping descent down a winding 3,600-ft. drop, known as the "Glass Elevator", all provide the variety of challenges that make the RAAM legendary among endurance cyclists.

I'm often asked in post-race conversations about the sights I saw, how the RAAM must have been a wonderful way to see the country. The disappointing truth is that sightseeing is definitely not one of the RAAM's attractions. I saw very little except for my ever-vigilant view of the road ahead. I saw *lots* of road kill -- snakes, turkeys, turtles, rabbits, raccoons, possums and even an armadillo, odd beast that he is. As far as experiencing the iconic American Landscape, I was either too busy avoiding the next rim-wrenching pothole or dead asleep in the RV to see but a disappointing number of those purple mountains' majesties and amber waves of grain.

Dur and I are awakened, dressed and anxious to ride an hour before Michael and Dave arrive in Brawley, CA for our first team exchange. Everyone is excited to see the racers arrive, especially Dur and me. Michael is on the last pull, and Dave is in the racer van with the driver and navigator. Everything about the exchange is so new and rushed that we don't get a chance to say much to each other. Someone hears Michael say, *"Goddamn, that was fun!"* when he's asked about his Glass Elevator ride, but at this point, that's as much as we know about the first 145 miles. These team exchanges are the RAAM's version of a NASCAR pit crew's chaotic work. Swapping drivers, navigators, bikes, clothing boxes, coolers, food and beverages involves a logistical choreography that leaves no time for chatter. A couple of minutes is all it takes. The race clock ticks and the hurry never stops when the crew and the team all converge in the exchange camp.

The official RAAM book of maps includes cross-section elevations of every mile of the route. Each page shows two of the 54 RAAM time stations, which range from about 30 to 90 miles apart. Race crews are required to check in by phone as they pass each station. The times are immediately uploaded onto RAAM's website, which is watched by team supporters all over the world, at all hours of the day and night. The maps' horizontal scale reads in miles, the vertical scale in ft. of elevation. The peaks and valleys sometimes look like erratic EKGs, sharp spikes and deep troughs.

Barney Brannen, racer RV driver/navigator

"First of all, calling this a 'camp' is definitely a misnomer. Our caravan is so itinerant, never sitting still for more than 3-4 hours, it would give a gypsy vertigo. But it's the closest we have to home base for our entire team of 4 racers and 15 crew members. The most important function camp fills is to provide a place for off-duty racers and crew to sleep and recharge before jumping back on duty. Every 8-9 hours, two racers will come off the course, get showered, massaged and fed, then popped into bed in our racer RV. At the same time, two of the on-course support crew, one from the racer van and one from the follow van, rotate out of their vehicles and into a flat (hopefully soft) spot in the crew RV

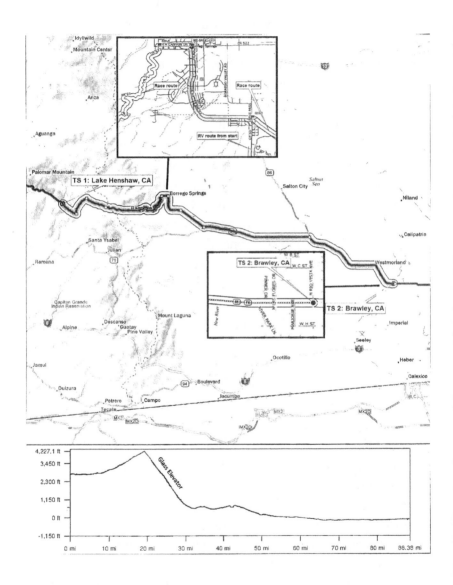

for a few hours of sleep. The rest of the crew catches a nap whenever time and space permit. In addition to being our traveling hotel, the crew camp also provides food, supplies, equipment and all other support needed to sustain four bicycle racers in continuous motion for a solid week. Each time the racers finish their 2-man, team exchange, the RVs pack up and move down the road to stage for the next team exchange, usually 150 miles +/- further along. We've staged in abandoned gas stations (coveted for their shade-offering canopies), gravelly desert washes and the parking lots of Wal-Mart, unofficial supply HQ for the RAAM.

A day for us in the racer RV goes like this: We roll into town, usually last, because, aside from the fact that Michael Scholl and I drive like little old ladies on the way to church, an attribute our occupants, at least, seem to appreciate, we wait for the racers who have just come off the course to go through their routines before we roll. A typical travel scenario will see two racers asleep in their bunks, Lydia Brewster, our soigneur nonpareil, trying to catch a few winks at the dinette table, and Michael Scholl or me at the wheel while the other navigates. When we reach the prearranged team exchange location, Michael and I will pull down our baseball caps, slouch into the RV's front seats and hope for a few overdue Zs. These brief respites end all too soon, when we get the call from the follow van that the racers on the road are 'an hour out'. These calls are the factory whistle for sleeping crew and racers in both RVs. Manny Casillas, our nutritionist, chef and stern team disciplinarian, cranks his kitchen into action to whip up a meal for the racers -- incoming and outgoing. Manny is usually assisted by Janice Smolowitz, who, as team nurse, we hope will have few calls for her professional skills. Before the in-coming racers arrive, the off-duty, racer van crew member will prepare the out-going racers' boxes. These boxes contain everything personal they'll need for the next 8 hours--extra clothes, an extra pair of shoes, two helmets (one time-trial helmet and one regular helmet), plus whatever assortment of energy powders, gels, electrolyte solutions, butt paste (chamois cream), etc. their particular racing regimens require. Someone else (typically me) will unlock and get off the RV rack all four of the out-going racers' bikes -- one TT bike and one road bike each and ready them for the day; check & fill tires; check to ensure headlights and taillights (all mandated by RAAM rules) are attached & functional, etc. One bike will go out on the road immediately with the first rider while the other three will be mounted on the racer van rack as soon as the in-coming racers' bikes are removed.

Meanwhile, Lydia readies her massage table, primarily to give the incoming racers a good rub down but often to loosen up stiff muscles for the guys getting ready to go out (and occasionally, if there's enough time and no immediate demand for her services, a special treat for one of the other crew members!). Other members of the crew check fluids in the vehicles and ready them for another leg on the road, clean up around camp and perform other duties as assigned. One or two other crew members walk the out-going racer and his bike to the edge of the road to await the in-coming's arrival.

According to RAAM rules, 'night' is defined as the hours between 7 p.m. and 7 a.m. RAAM rules require crew members to wear head lamps, yellow reflective vests and ankle straps during these hours to minimize the possibility of roadside collisions. Also, incoming riders must come to a complete stop before the out-going rider departs, whereas during 'daylight' hours, the racers may execute rolling transitions in order to minimize loss of time. Additionally, racers cannot ride even a few feet down the course at night without the follow van and the bright illumination of its headlights immediately behind. When the follow van is swapping out its crew and provisions, and the out-going racer must wait until the swap is complete, the delay is frustrating, even in a race expected to take a week."

It's 11 p.m. We're 145 miles from the start when the racing begins for Dur and me. He takes the first pull on his TT bike, and speeds away locked into the headlights of the follow van. I'm in the racer van with the driver and navigator. As we leapfrog past Dur a mile down the road, I shout encouragement out the window. *The RAAM is on!* In twenty minutes, it will be my turn on the bike and Dur's turn to rest, a pattern we plan to repeat all the way to Annapolis. For now, we're ready to ride all night, 141 miles to our scheduled team exchange in Parker, AZ.

Dur Higgins
"Night riding was something I had long dreaded because we had not done any night training, and I had it in my mind that visibility would be poor, nocturnal animals would run in front of us, Saturday night drunk drivers would be on the road late, etc. But our first night shift was GREAT! We were in the flat desert with a tailwind on straight roads with smooth pavement. Add a TT bike, helmet and skin suit, and you are sailing. Don and I flew that night!"

It's dark, and we have no idea of the landscape unfolding around us. California or Ohio? We could be anywhere. Our route is well-paved, with long flat stretches and moderate hills. It seems to me we are riding very fast, easily exceeding our target average of 18 mph. I've ridden often at night before, but never for such long distances at such high speeds, never bathed in the high-beamed glare of a following vehicle. Night rides in the woods and in 24-

hour mountain bike races were illuminated by a single, helmet-mounted lamp, good enough light at low speeds, but nothing so luminous as this. And we need all the visibility we can get. During this month of June, 2012, the moon will be dark on the 19th and 20th, precisely midway through the RAAM. If there are stars, I don't see them, but only for fear of lifting my eyes too far above the road.

At the top of a long climb, 40-some miles out of Brawley, we come to a US Border Patrol Inspection Station (Mexico is 20 miles to the south). I instinctively dislike and distrust gun-toting authority, but my distrust turns to shame when the conspicuously Latino officers politely wave us through. A single glance at my Caucasian complexion, exotic cycling ensemble and RAAM follow van leads them to conclude we're no threat to National Border Security, and away we go, reverse-profiled. Reminding myself that the justice of American politics is not on my list of things to rectify tonight, I bear down hard on my pedals.

Howard Conway, crew RV driver/navigator

"I have worked for Ford Motor Credit Co. for 32 years, moved several times to keep the job, worked in at least 20+ different jobs while at Ford Credit. My hobby is people. I have worked and played, coached and supervised, observed and interacted with thousands of people in my life, and I am always trying to figure them out, see what makes them tick. It's a slow dance working and observing people, but it is very interesting.

Speaking with my old college buddy, Dave Eldridge, a year before the 2012 RAAM, I told him I would like to make the trip with him sometime. I didn't own or ride a bike and had no idea what I was getting into, but I knew I could work hard, interact with and lead people, so I thought this would be a fun way to see the country between San Diego,

CA and Annapolis, MD. Boy, was I ever wrong about seeing anything! It was all a blur for 6 + days.

Before we left Oceanside, I tried to observe and figure out who was who among the crew. We had one guy wearing black toe nail polish, so man, who knew what kind of guy he was? The crew tried to get to know the riders and each other, but it was hard, everyone being so busy. The racers were consumed with getting ready to race, but I think some of the crew took that to mean they were a bit aloof, and the first little signs of tension began to show."

We ride fast along some smooth, flat stretches before we cross the Colorado River, somewhere between Blythe, CA and Parker, AZ. This once great river, mighty enough to carve out the Grand Canyon, is so diminished by agricultural and drinking water needs upstream that the bridge we cross is barely distinguishable from the highway. The sign marking the river is equally diminished and obscure, as if embarrassed by how little river flow remains.

I feel grateful and safe hearing the follow-van's steady purr behind me while its headlights cast my shadow on the road ahead. The van's headlights create a stereoscopic image on the pavement: I'm perpetually riding towards two, elongated, shadow representations of myself, legs churning in perfect synchronicity. The van is outfitted with rear-facing, blinking lights on its roof and a large, yellow warning sign, CAUTION BICYCLES AHEAD. From a safety standpoint, the follow van drivers /navigators, John Markley, Ken Gunnells and mechanic Greg Thompson, perform the crew's most important assignment: protecting the racers from rear-end collisions. They do, indeed, *have our backs*. Rotating through their 16-hour shifts in the tortoise-paced follow van has got to be the most hypnotically boring job on Earth. Imagine these gallant volunteers, driving 3,000 miles at less than 20 mph. Additionally, imagine that their slow-motion perspective of America the Beautiful is never far from either side of an old guy's spandexed butt.

Dur and I have been out for 4-5 hours, and I feel strong. The pavement ahead seems like an endless spool, forever unreeling away from me. I keep burrowing into the tunnel of light, and it seems as if my bicycle has become an integral part of my body. The night air smells like creosote and mesquite, then I'm hit with the pungent reminder of roadside cattle. My mind is excited but oddly empty. There's a keen awareness of the pavement's surface and the occasional night creature darting across my path, a bird, a mouse, the reflection from a coyote's eyes. The only demands of the universe are reduced to this speeding down the road. The simplicity of it all is as intoxicatingly glamorous as it is surprisingly relaxing.

I'm pedaling my TT bike down a long stretch of smooth, fast road when I see, in the distance, a RAAM follow van's signature, blinking caution lights, and realize I'm catching up to someone racing the RAAM. The thrilling *necessity* of catching and passing a distant racer is every cyclist's instinctive, reflexive *duty*, to which, I confess, I'm not immune. I compress my torso into an even lower aero tuck and increase my pedal stroke by another few beats. Drafting is not allowed in the RAAM, and I momentarily worry about the logistics of getting by the rider's follow van -- *and* the rider -- without appearing to take advantage of their drafts. But as I close in, I find there will be no question that I am indeed *passing*, not drafting. My teammates and I will each pass a couple of teams' racers during the RAAM, but the permanent sorting out of slower or faster is mostly complete within the first 300 miles.

Our schedule calls for a team exchange with Michael

and Dave in Parker, AZ but when Dur and I are individually in the racer van, Taylor and Chris break some unexpected news: "You can go another 56 miles to Salome, right?" The remark is more rhetorical than interrogative, but we're both having a great ride, and at this early stage in the race, we'll agree to do whatever is needed without asking why. (Dur is told that the reason for the extended shift is that we have ridden so fast that our portion would bring us in much too early.) Whatever the reason may be, we ride 197 miles to Salome on our first RAAM pull instead of the 141 to Parker, as scheduled -- close to 10 hours in the saddles. It's been a long night, but it's our first, and despite the extended shift, we're excited.

From the RAAM route book

"There are limited 24-hour services from Time Station 4 in Parker AZ to Time Station 7 in Prescott. Crews needing provisions for the next 150 miles may want to take advantage of the Wal-Mart Supercenter always open at 100 Riverside Drive. Go straight for .5 miles instead of turning at 04E-R."

Approaching Salome, we pass the tiny settlement of Hope, AZ. population unspecified on the modest sign by the road. Most of Hope is apparently transient, gathered up in long rows in a big RV park. A few miles later, the follow-van headlights illuminate another roadside sign that reads, "YOUR NOW BEYOND HOPE." The sign keeps me alternately smiling at the use of bad grammar and wondering if the sign's message should be interpreted as a cautionary prophecy.

I grind the last leg of our shift up a long, uphill grade. I'm tired and glad it's almost over. The night riding was thrilling, but the hours just before sunrise are unusually difficult. Even on a flat road with a tail wind or a downhill run, that pre-dawn interlude reminds our bodies of their interrupted circadian rhythms and low levels of cortisol, a combination that drains away energy and gathers up negative thoughts. But as the first hint of daylight stains the sky, I feel an uncanny sense of rejuvenation. I'm looking forward to seeing the crew and exchanging war stories, telling them about the enormous rattlesnake I saw squashed in the road and almost ran over. I pick up speed with inexplicably freshened legs and crest the hill straight into a gigantic orange disc rising over the horizon.

At the team exchange in Salome, AZ, we are 342 miles into the race and averaging 19.88 mph, well above our 18 mph target, despite almost 9,500 ft. of accumulated climbing since sea level at Oceanside. The team exchange isn't quite the frenzied swap it was the first time, but it's still all about hustle. I come in and Michael takes off; that's all I know. I don't see Dave Burnett, but I'm too tired and self-absorbed to wonder why.

Barney Brannen

"What makes this the 'World's toughest bicycle race' is not that one, or two, or four, or even eight riders have to string together continuous rides for 3,000 miles -- that's a given, a known, a monumental but surmountable challenge. What makes this race so damned tough is that all the training, preparation and planning in the world can never adequately anticipate or plan for the inevitable fact that something will go wrong that you hadn't planned for. Our crew chief invested untold hours in planning, planning, planning for every racer exchange, every team exchange and every driver exchange, plus all the meal prep, fuel stops, massaging, laundry, showering, bike swapping & fixing that has to go off like clockwork to complete this

race at a record-breaking pace. Elaborate, multi-page, multi-color, multi-level schedules promise to befuddle but, ultimately, deliver the goods. Then, in one fell swoop, we can be at 'Plan B', which is: 'Makin' it up as we go along!'

In Brawley, CA, following the end of his and Michael's first shift, Dave Burnett fell ill. Our crew chief and RN made a quick and wise decision: move everyone down the road to the next scheduled team exchange in Parker, AZ. There's a hospital in Parker, and if Dave isn't better by then, they'll have him admitted -- which they ultimately do. Meanwhile, they have Dur and Don extend their shift 56 miles past Parker to Salome, AZ, another 2-1/2 hours.

As we approach Salome, AZ, Dave still isn't back from the hospital, and Dur and Don are due to arrive. They've already spent much more time on the road than we planned or they anticipated. What do we do? We don't dare squeeze any more out of them, but we can't sit still either, so we send out Michael, the one healthy, rested racer we have left, and hope he can ride solo for 50-some miles, about three hours, a lot of it <u>uphill</u>. The premise is that he can pace himself into a long pull rather than riding the intense 20-30 minute shifts planned, and that an easier pace will allow him some reasonable rest and recovery. Then, so we don't completely incinerate Michael, we will send out Don to give Michael some relief. The only problem is that Don has already got more than two extra hours in his legs and will have only three hours off the bike, which means maybe he'll get an hour+ of sleep, if he's lucky."

While Dur takes a shower, I hobble over to Lydia 's massage table and apologize for being crusty with road grime and RAAM B.O. Married to a former motocross motorcyclist, Lydia knows all about grime and sweat, and couldn't care less. As I melt into the luxury of her strong hands, I ask about her RAAM affiliation, and learn Lydia is a rookie, a friend and admirer of Michael and Elena Patterson, and I get that she is as supportive of the cause as she is bemused by its motivation. She's clearly earnest in seeing to it that the racers' bodies function at maximum efficiency, while her lack of enthusiasm for the kind of knuckleheaded ambition the RAAM demands is something she graciously declines to discuss. Lydia seems to have an intuitive sensitivity to cyclists' tender spots. Before I can think to mention a region of a tight quadriceps, she finds it and kneads it back into shape. Lying on my stomach while she teases out the gremlins lurking in my hamstrings, I feel as if I can tell her anything and it will be received with good will and compassion.

Dur gets on the table next. I shower, change clothes and eat a few bowls of chef Manny Casillas's turkey pasta, washed down with a strawberry-banana smoothie. Perfect. Manny is never without his red headband, which becomes a sort of RAAM talisman for me. He is so solicitous of his racers that I'm initially embarrassed by his attentiveness. I've never been treated so well. While I'm eating, I use Barney's cell phone to call my wife Melinda. She's been eagerly following Barney's RAAM-bling blog as well as the RAAM website. Like Lydia, this cross-country escapade is far beyond Melinda's definition of sanity, but she has been resolutely supportive and is so glad to hear from me I choke up with gratitude. I avoid mentioning fatigue or the extra mileage we've just been asked to ride, but am happy to emphasize how great the crew is. As if to prove it, Manny comes over with a plastic chair and leads me to the shade of a warehouse, where he hectors me to sit, and *don't waste energy standing in the sun even if I am talking to my sweetheart!* Manny is a RAAM veteran, an energetic guy in his 30's who knows his stuff. In 3,000 miles, whatever hour of the day or night, I never once see him without his signature red headband, preparing food for the team-exchange meals, putting together the endless snacks for the racer van cooler, always busy.

Sitting pretty in Manny's shaded chair, I babble on to Melinda -- what a thrilling night ride we had, and how safe it was with the follow-van behind us -- all true. I reassure her that those many hours stolen from us while I was training all winter are paying off. She's relieved to hear the good news and -- I hope -- a little less anxious about the toll this race will take on her husband, who is 15 years older than she. Before I hang up, I say two things I mean with all my heart: "I love you," and, "I promise I'll make it home to you safe and sound."

Dave Burnett's wife, Nancy, writes about Dave

"David, at the age of 52, was skiing with our 14 yr-old son, Andrew. At the top of Jay Peak's steepest mountain he challenged Andrew to a race to the bottom. When they were near the end David went into a tuck, and his ski hit some ice. He was thrown into a railroad tie implanted in the snow, and broke his tibia and fibula, fractured his pelvis and dislocated his hip. His first words were: "I think I broke my hip." His second: "But I was ahead of him when I crashed!" Followed by; "I guess I won't be running the Burlington (VT) Marathon this summer."

I include the above as an example of David's competitive nature. We've been married for 35 years, so I was not surprised when he told me he was going to compete in the RAAM. Nor was I surprised by the single-mindedness and intensity of his training, because I doubted the race could be much more arduous than the regimen he followed to prepare. He'd emerge from the basement after 6 continuous hours on his trainer, or ride up (barely) our long, 16% grade driveway after a ride, and look more exhausted than I'd ever seen him. The actual race, therefore, was a bit of an anti-climax. I knew he'd be receiving wonderful support from Dave Eldridge and his teammates and crew, and I hoped his riding in a large, organized event would be safer than many of his training rides, fighting with cars, dogs and narrow or nonexistent bike lanes. I wasn't entirely surprised when he pushed himself so hard that he ended up in a hospital, dehydrated and weakened on the first day of the race."

Dur and I have been in our bunks for what seems like mere minutes when our crew chief comes into the RV. I feel a tug on my foot, and after a moment of disorientation, I am wide awake and looking straight into the face of Dave Eldridge. Dave is a younger, Kenny Rogers look-alike. While he exudes a solid, professional competence and a *get-'er-done* attitude, he also has a ready sense of humor. Ever since we first met in Tucson during team training camp, he and I have joked around a lot. I'm used to a Dave Eldridge with a ready quip and a wide smile, but now, his expression is somber. "We had to take Burnett to the hospital."

Racer van driver/navigator Chris Champion

"I was amazed by the show of endurance that Dave and Michael put in climbing over Mount Palomar. Despite the climbs, we were averaging over 20mph since Lake Henshaw. Then Dave began burping. He was drinking Gatorade, and since I could never stand Gatorade, I surmised that he had some kind of acid stomach reflux. He kept riding hard, but eating little. Not that he didn't try - but everything he ate seemed to make his stomach worse. We didn't know what to do but try to give him salty snacks and make sure he was hydrated. More burps.

Then burps became 'vurps', that nasty combination of vomit and burp. Dave was still burping hard when we arrived at the scheduled team exchange in Parker, where he became very ill and was rushed to the hospital."

The enormity of the implications take only a moment to absorb. It will be impossible to set a record with only three racers. Our great beginnings, our huge potential, the lofty goal embraced by 19 of us out here on the road, plus the expectations of our enthusiastic friends and loved ones -- and generous sponsor -- all of that is at serious risk less than 24 hours from the start. I'm told Dave has been released from the hospital, but he's still shaky, needs some rest. I wonder where they find even an aspirin out in this remote desert country, then learn that the regional hospital in Parker is 10 minutes off the race route. As it happens, there are no other patients in the Emergency Room and the staff is waiting out on the tarmac when Dave arrives. Talk about good luck following bad! "What about Michael?" I wonder aloud. "If Dave is out of the loop . . . ?"

Our crew chief is uneasy. "Michael has been out there alone for almost 3 hours," he says. I'm still draped over the edge of my bunk, half-dressed and sorting out my thoughts when he adds, "I need you out there *now."* At the other end of the RV, Dur has been unable to sleep, and has overheard the conversation. It's understood that I will go out first and Dur will follow in an hour or two. I'm hastily pulling on a fresh kit when Dave Burnett steps up into the RV.

We immediately see he is wobbly on his feet, ashen, haggard -- and mortified. With an ideal cyclist's build at 5'-11", 140 lbs, Dave is a fierce competitor with huge talents and a long list of bicycle race victories to prove it. This sudden state of helplessness is difficult territory for him. An irrepressible leader of any peloton, Dave would often pull ahead on team training rides, flying away in a surge of unfettered pleasure in the ability to go fast, fast, fast. *"I can't help myself,"* he'd say when we'd catch up and caution him that we still had many miles to go. *"I know,"* he'd say. *"I have to control myself, but it's really hard."*

Racer van driver/navigator Nate Keck

"As we were passing through the Anza Borrego desert, Dave was making every effort possible to remain hydrated in the 100+-degree heat and low humidity. From an exercise physiologist's perspective, it was the classic case of dehydration combined with forced re-hydration that leads to an electrolyte imbalance, which then causes vomiting and an even more severe dehydration."

Dave Burnett

"In the early hours of the first day, it became clear to me that my only job was to ride and take care of my rest, nutrition and cleanliness. I had neither the time, the energy nor the expertise to deal with the RAAM's complex organizational issues, and it seemed there was no need for me to think or even talk: everything logistic would be managed by our knowledgeable crew. It felt appropriate to think of myself as simply a piece of meat, best suited to ride and shut up.

As the hours of that first shift proceeded, my recollections of the terrain, the hour of the day and the temperature became a blur. I just rode as hard as I could and let the guys in the racer van tell me what bike to use and when to be ready for my next pull. I had designed my own nutrition plan which relied heavily on supplemental nutritional products, rather than standard, everyday foods. This approach had worked successfully for me in all my previous, day-racing experiences, but now in the racer RV, I began vomiting up everything in my stomach. My solution was to eat even more of my favorite electrolyte drinks and nutritional products. It didn't work. I vomited again and again and then curled up in the back of the RV and sought refuge in sleep. With no idea of time or mission, I was lost in a vague, dreamlike/awake state. I remember thinking, "I wonder if this is what it feels like to die?" I was perfectly comfortable with this thought, and I was, indeed, thinking that death was a real possibility. There was absolutely no alarm or panic. I was completely at ease with where I was and the prospect of death. I'm embarrassed to admit (and this thought brings tears to my eyes today) that I had no thoughts about getting word to my family that I loved them or that they had been the most wonderful thing that had happened to me in my life (as I write this, I have so many tears in my eyes that I can't find the keys). I was just plain comfortable. I wouldn't call it bliss, but it felt like extreme comfort just to lie there and do nothing.

My second recollection was seeing crew chief Dave Eldridge looking down on me and telling me in a very supportive manner that he was going to take me to the hospital. I followed him and Karen Scheerer to their van and off we went. I remember our arrival at a very small medical facility where it seemed to me that they were ready for me. After a very quick blood test I had a needle in my arm within minutes and was given the first of 3 liters (almost 7 lbs) of IV fluids. This gradually led to clearer thoughts and a trip back to the RV and a deep sleep. I still have no idea how long I slept or how long this whole incapacitation process took me, but I do remember to my great pleasure that when I rejoined the rotation with Michael Paterson I was feeling very strong. I have much gratitude toward my teammates for their perseverance while I was incapacitated and for those who cared for me and made decisions about my care, all of which may have saved my life."

Dehydration is a cyclist's sneakiest foe. As the body perspires in response to exercise, perspiration vanishes into the air so invisibly that the cyclist is unaware of how much fluid is being lost. This evaporative cooling effect is doubly insidious in hotter, dryer environments. The standard cyclists' warning about hydration is: *If you wait until you're thirsty, it's too late.* Trainers recommend an average of at least 20 oz. of replacement fluid every hour during intense exercise, and considerably more in extreme temperatures.

"I'm sorry, guys," Dave says, grasping at the RV's dinette table to keep his balance. "I feel terrible about this . . ." We hasten to reassure him, *don't worry about it, we'll make it work.*

"I kept throwing up . . ." He opens his eyes wide and nods his head slowly, "I thought this was it, guys. I really did."

It's painful to see Dave so shaken, so embarrassed about something he never meant to happen. We encourage him to relax, drink and eat real food and get some sleep, take the time to do whatever it takes to get better. We want him to believe -- we want *ourselves* to believe he'll be back in the game in no time. But as I put on my shoes, I can't help but wonder: *will he?* Could a 3-man team make it to Annapolis -- forget the record -- in any sort of respectable time, or are we irreversibly screwed?

I hurriedly mix supplements in two water bottles, gather up optional riding gear and gobble an energy bar. The sun is already blazing hot, and I sleepily dither about whether I should wear a white, featherweight, long-sleeved jersey to help reflect sunlight from my arms. I finally decide, yes, and then realize that the amount of effort it took to reach this trivial decision is indicative of my weariness. I'm glad I got to speak to Melinda when I did, because at the moment, she'd hear the fatigue in my voice. Meanwhile, the crew has my TT bike ready to roll and are generous with their encouragements, but I know they are wondering and worrying, too.

Dur Higgins

"We were told we were moving the exchange 56 miles further east because we were going so fast. I was going fast, and because we went so much farther than our scheduled 141 miles, I was starting to feel cramps coming on. I had to be careful getting into the racer van each time to keep my hamstrings from locking up when I curled my legs. When we got to camp, I showered, got my much-needed massage, ate, and went to bed, but I could not sleep. There were crew persons in and around the RV talking a lot, and I could hear just enough to add to my concern about what was happening. I heard Don in the next room preparing to go out early to take over for Michael who had been out for 3 hours solo."

The crew hustles me into the van and we speed up the road to find Michael. After a dozen miles or so, we spot him near the town of Congress, working hard up a grade, his trademark red cycling shoes spinning a healthy cadence. He looks composed and steady despite his 3-hour, 50+ mile effort, which far exceeds the length of a single pull any of us will ride in the RAAM. Who would guess this was a 70-year-old cyclist? Who could imagine he was in Oceanside, California less than 24 hours ago? As we connect at the exchange, I can see he's weary, but also calm and confident as usual. We have no time to speak more than a few words. Michael is a naturally reserved, modest person, but he graciously thanks me for coming out to spell him, while I insist it's *he* who deserves credit for taking on such a huge section by himself; all of this is communicated in about the same time it takes to read this sentence.

Platitudes about the benefits of team work may be generically applicable, but most of the RAAM format leaves us riding and resting in isolation. Dur and I already feel team-ish, but we only get to know one another during the brief intervals when we're not riding or sleeping, We see Michael and Dave for only a few hurried minutes every 8-9 hours and have no way of knowing how they're doing or what they're thinking. This exchange with Michael is one of the few times that the personification of "team" feels palpable: We are counting on each other in dire circumstances and delivering what is needed. Before I take off up the Yarnell Grade, I notice a crust of salt staining Michael's helmet strap and imagine the gallons of fluids he must have consumed to keep himself moving in such demanding circumstances. I've known Michael just long enough to know his determination, discipline and toughness run deep; this brief encounter in Arizona confirms it all: The Sultan of Cycling is showing his stuff.

From the RAAM route book
". . . The Yarnell Grade climbs 1,800 feet in 7 miles. From mile 27.5 . . . until you get to Prescott mountain, driving will be treacherous! Averaging more than 130 feet (of elevation) per mile, this is the most difficult climbing west of Maryland."

The first few miles of my pull out of Congress are pug-ugly. The difficulty of getting any speed out of these straight, empty miles is demoralizing, the opposite of last night's rock and roll glory. In the heat-shimmering distance, I see that the road swings right and I can make out guardrails

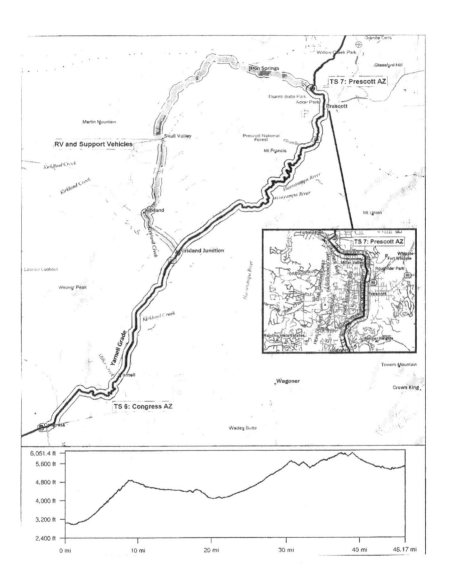

along the near edge of a steeper grade that appears to go on forever. The air out here is scented with the stringent perfume of 110-degree asphalt and, what, *sagebrush?* Alien odors to this indigenous Yankee. Unlike New Hampshire's densely wooded slopes, these mountains are vast and barren, striped with sloping geological strata that deceive the eye and confuse assumptions about what is horizontal. There is no reliable reference for *level* here. What exactly is the grade I'm climbing, or, am I climbing at all? It looks flattish, but I know it's supposed to be at least 5 %, and it feels like 10 %. *Am I too tired to know the difference?*

Michael and I have traded 5 or 6 pulls when crew chief Dave and Karen Scheerer whiz past with Dur in the van. They will take Michael back to the Mother Ship for much-deserved rest and sleep and leave Dur and me to finish the rotation into Prescott. What I don't know is that we've just conquered the legendary Yarnell Grade, which must be why my aching legs cause me to wonder, *are we going to have to call it quits if Dave can't recover? Or, are we going to have to call it quits because I can't recover?* And now the shadow I'm casting over our likelihood of success is also casting a shadow over my befuddled logic: if the RAAM goes from west to east and it's late morning, my shadow should be behind me, to my left. But I see my shadow ahead of me to my left. What is going on? I'm too tired to think out of the west-to-east box, but later, in a more coherent moment, I'll look at a map and see that for 30 miles we were travelling almost due north despite our inevitably eastward route.

Janice Smolowitz, RN/nurse practitioner

"Why me? I'd be the last person expected to take part in an endurance event, especially as a crew member on the RAAM. My idea of cycling involves riding my 20 year-old,

40 pound, lime green cruiser with foot brakes on the trails near my house, solely for the purpose of watching a sunset. But I'd heard of the RAAM and wondered what kind of people participated, so there I was leaving Oceanside, CA on June 16th, looking forward to seeing what I'd got myself into.

Since 1982, I have been employed as a nurse practitioner, and presently provide patient care, teach, and have administrative responsibilities at Columbia University School of Nursing. Early in January 2012, Michael Patterson invited me to join the RAAM team. While intriguing, the idea seemed completely insane and was far removed from my comfort zone as a health care professional. Nevertheless, I agreed to speak with Dave Eldridge, and he told me about his son and experience with RAAM as well as the Run Across America. I tried to be as honest as possible and explained I was not an endurance enthusiast or sports medicine specialist, but I could refer friends who worked in orthopedics and emergency rooms who were ideal candidates. By the time we finished speaking, I was hooked and reasonably terrified. For the next six months, I would awaken nightly from a dream that involved serious injury to someone that I would attribute to my own lack of knowledge about extreme sports.

Dave suggested I contact Karen Scheerer, who was amazing. She was easy going and a very calming influence. I asked Karen if I should watch the film, 'Bicycle Dreams'. She didn't think it was a good idea, and, in retrospect I agree. I asked if we needed oxygen, intravenous fluids, or suture material and she replied, 'Just think boo-boos and band aids.' Ultimately she was right, but I was not going to stop worrying and preparing. I read numerous cycling books written by exercise physiologists and sports *physicians. The reading was useful in preparing the medical kits that would travel with the riders and crew. I was able to anticipate certain situations and include items that might be needed. I also began mapping a previous RAAM route to identify and record contact information for all emergency rooms.*

I drove friends and colleagues crazy. John Violante, paramedic and the simulation director at the School came to work early to practice road side trauma scenarios with me. He regularly emailed me the question of the day. My personal favorite was, 'The RAAM crew decides to have lunch in a field while waiting for the riders. Five hours later, crew members begin complaining of headaches, difficulty thinking clearly, vomiting, diarrhea, sweating, anxiety, and respiratory symptoms. What are you going to do?' The answer was acute organophosphate poisoning due to insecticides sprayed on the field and treatment involved atropine. I also heard how, in previous RAAMs, close quarters had serious, negative impacts, causing respiratory and gastrointestinal illnesses. Environmental preventive measures would be paramount. While it was unlikely this would happen, I found myself monitoring where food was being consumed throughout the race. Antiseptic wipes became my best friend. I was actually pleased to be assisting Manny, our chef. As a vegan, I wasn't sure how I would figure out if food prepared for racers would be palatable, but I knew we would be working on clean surfaces. It was only after the racers crossed over Wolf Creek Pass that I began to calm down and appreciate the gift of the journey.

The racer RV drivers were more conservative than the crew RV drivers. Eventually, I developed confidence and began to feel like I had inherited a bunch of younger brothers. At times, I felt myself saying things I had said to my sons when they started driving. Luckily, the crew RV drivers ignored my comments or found innovative ways to keep me quiet. For example, as we climbed the Yarnell Grade between Congress and Prescott Arizona, at the point where our map described this as the most treacherous driving west of Maryland, resting crew members insisted I look out the window overlooking the cliff and repeatedly requested our driver pull over so I could see the vehicles that had fallen off, crashed and burned. A day or two later, as we descended the Cucharra Pass summit with its 6% grade, I recall asking the driver, Lewis, who had a military background, if he could slow down. The response was, 'Jan stop worrying. We're driving a tank without a cannon. It's riding fine. Let's forget the directions and go climb that mountain over there. Looks like a good view.' At that moment, I began laughing and the trip took on a whole new meaning.

There were many times during the RAAM when I couldn't imagine how the riders were accomplishing their task, but the fact that they did was inspiring. I'm glad I was offered the opportunity to come along for the ride, and I appreciate the generosity of spirit and sharing I found. It was definitely the adventure of a lifetime, and it was reassuring to learn I could live without porcelain and function 'somewhat' on two hours of sleep in twenty-four."

The three women on our team are as resilient and resourceful as they are indispensable. Nurse Jan administers to boo-boos, wards off the infamous scourges of RAAM life in close quarters and helps Manny keep us nourished. Lydia Brewster incessantly restores incessantly sore muscles, and Karen Scheerer is the team shepherdess, multi-tasker, photographer, Uber Mom and problem solver.

At rider exchanges, she is the first to inquire about any special needs the racers may have -- and makes sure they are met. Her smile is all-natural, organic, free-range sincere. And now, as the van passes me on the way to Prescott, she leans out the window with her camera and shouts some high-pitched encouragement. *Did she say I was doing great?* How did she know that was just what I needed to hear out here on this goddamned endless, sun-bleached mountainside in the middle of nowhere? I don't care if she's lying through her pretty white teeth. It's what I needed -- whatever it was she said, it *sounded* like she said I was doing great and I'm taking her at her word, *whatever* it was. It's ridiculous, how so little from the right person can mean so much at the right time, but it works. Vanity restored, ego boosted and mood repaired, I double down on the pedals. I'm doing great: *Karen said so.* I'm probably going no faster, but my attitude lifts and I have an epiphany: Dave's crisis is what makes this adventure an *adventure.* Without the unexpected, this RAAM would feel like a week's worth of tedious math: 458 miles x 6.55 days = Oceanside to Annapolis, equation complete, class dismissed. I never liked math precisely because of its unconditional rectitude, and if we had no bumps in this RAAMroad, it would be math class all over again. So, the question isn't how many miles are we riding, but what will happen to make some of those miles more memorable than others. Obsessing about what was *supposed* to be is asking for boredom. I'm sorry for Dave's suffering and would never have wished it upon any of us, but this has turned into the kind of adventure I wanted to have -- not just challenging, but *unpredictably* challenging. I'll ride as hard as I can, but what happens beyond that is beyond my control. Epiphany complete, I'm ready to keep humping the bike up the hill and embrace the adventure of unpredictability.

Dave Eldridge

"My job as crew chief is like conducting an orchestra. I don't play the instruments, I make sure the players play them according to the score. There's no place for soloists on a winning RAAM team, no room for prima donnas. What makes a team successful is when everybody does their job and everybody uses the words, Can I help?, please, and thank you, as often as possible. Teamwork is the key to success on a RAAM campaign, and it looked from the start as if we had put together an excellent crew. Now all we needed was for the racers to do their part and see how fast we could get to Annapolis.

The day-to-day, ups and downs of the individual racers and crew are covered elsewhere in this book, so I don't need to repeat what's already been covered, but what I can add, is my management approach to the unpredictable aspects of the race. Experience has taught me what to expect in different parts of the country under normal circumstances, such as where the racers are likely to go the fastest, go the slowest, get optimistic or pessimistic or even collapse. Those parts are predictable, but if we get thrown a curve ball, everything changes. For instance, when a serious medical event occurs, specific feedback from the crew in the racer van allows me to make an informed decision on what to do next. What I found from Day One on was that the racers and the crew were adaptable to unexpected changes, which they made without blame or complaint, very professional. The welcome surprise was that after the first 56 hilly miles at the start, our accumulated average speed never dropped below 18.35 mph, even with one racer missing from Parker to Tuba City. All along the way, every report from every time station gave a huge boost to the crew and team's spirits. The 18 mph average I set as a worthy target made our actual progress seem spectacular, and the farther we went, we all began to realize we could put something in the record books that would be there for a long time. I'm glad Michael Patterson called me, and I'm proud of the work the crew and the racers put into making the 2012 RAAM such a success. I've even thought a few times since about getting on a bike myself, but that's another story yet to be told."

At time station # 7 in Prescott AZ, T430's accumulated average speed is 19.08 mph.

"Growing old is mandatory. Growing up is optional."

Anonymous

DAY TWO
Prescott, AZ to Pagosa Springs, CO
471 miles

The second 24 hours of our race calendar begins in Prescott, AZ, 441 miles from the start. By midday, Dur and I have shared about 35 miles since we relieved Michael on the Yarnell Grade. We're averaging less than 16 mph due to the climbing and lack of sleep. After the Yarnell summit at 5,100 ft., we rode 30 miles of flattish terrain, then crested a 6,100-ft. peak before descending down into Prescott at elevation 5,300. Preparing for the RAAM last winter, we had concerns about the effects of high-altitude riding, which now seem unwarranted. As far as we can tell, none of us have suffered from the enervating effects of thin air, especially Dave Burnett who slept -- alone, his wife pointedly notes -- in a hyperbaric tent for 6 months before the race, prompting his body to build extra red blood cells. Some endurance athletes deliberately relocate to, and train at high altitudes in order to gain a competitive edge in races at lower altitudes. Leading up to the start of the RAAM, Dave had raised his oxygen-content level to an equivalent of 13,000 ft. of elevation.

Howard Conway

"My expectations for sightseeing across America on the RAAM disappeared on Day One, but on Day Two, there were a few sights I never expected to see anywhere. In Prescott, we were set up for the rider exchange in a Wal-Mart parking lot below a ridge with houses on it. Some long haired guy was sitting on the edge of the deck of his house watching the world go by. A little later, a nice looking woman came out and sat beside him. We didn't think any more about it,

and then one of our guys said, hey, look up there, and the couple was in the midst of making out and really getting after it. Then in a few minutes she goes down on her knees and unzips his pants and proceeds right there in front of Wal-Mart and our entire Crew. It was interesting, how the women on the crew turned their heads away, and the guys kept peeking up, trying not to stare. Then the racers arrived and it was time to get back to work."

As the workday wears on into the afternoon, our pace picks up and I find myself cautiously, stupidly, *unbelievably* believing I feel pretty good. I even dare think that my months of training and the excitement of the RAAM will reveal that I'm a person who can ride this kind of volume on a few winks of sleep. Why not? Reto Schoch, the winner of this year's men's solo event, will average 15.08 mph on 2 hours of sleep out of every 24, so, why can't I? *Because he's younger than your youngest child?* Even imagining that I can somehow imitate the slowest of the *slow* solo riders is as dangerous and tantalizing as it is absurdly self-aggrandizing. This naive delusion continues for the next several hours until it's betrayed by the ruthless realities of Oak Creek Canyon.

From Prescott, Dur and I are facing another full rotation of 166-miles. We've barely rested since our first rotation of 197 miles, but now we're on to Cottonwood, Sedona and Flagstaff, eventually ending at the team exchange in Tuba City, AZ where Michael and Dave will take on the next rotation to Montezuma Creek, UT.

The first 25 miles east of Prescott dip and then climb 1,300 ft. on a gentle grade. Dur takes the first 6-7 miles, I go next, and Dur finishes his second pull near the 7,000 ft. Hickey Mountain summit. The next 15 miles descend 3,700 ft. through the old mining town of Jerome, and down into Cottonwood. The long, fast descent just happens to be on my dance card. I feel a bit guilty that Dur doesn't get to ride it with me, but since a regular rider rotation is essential to our rest and recovery, there is no choice about who will ride a specific section. Luckily, as a team, we are reasonably similar riders in any terrain and preferences don't matter; we stick to the schedule and ride what needs to be ridden when the clock says it's our turn to ride. Sometimes we get lucky. Sometimes we don't.

I'm feeling *extra* lucky as I fly down towards Jerome at 45 mph. The road is smooth, the curves are wide and the air rushing by is energizing. I know Jerome is near when tourist traffic begins to thicken and maintaining speed becomes a challenge. Our follow van is required to detour this section due to Jerome's half-mile of congestion, so I'm on my worst, unobserved behavior as I pin-ball through slow-moving vehicles and squeak past large pedestrians eating even larger ice cream cones. I pass a Volvo with an open window and wish the driver a nice day. I swerve to avoid a suddenly opened SUV door and let loose a choice Anglo-Saxon expletive. This dodge-ball-on-a-bike through Jerome is physically effortless but mentally challenging, and it boosts my confidence: on Day Two of the RAAM, I can still ride fast and think straight and have fun, all at the same time -- as long as it's downhill.

Below the clutter of traffic in Jerome, the road is empty and gravity makes life enjoyably simple. I have full use of the road width and am able to pick perfect lines through a couple of hairpin turns and a bunch of left-right wiggles. The object here is to prepare the route through the turn as the straightest line possible: come in wide on the outside, hug the inside (the apex) and follow through to the outside again. These high-speed turns require weight on the outside pedal at the 6 o'clock position and a slight pressure on the inside bar end. Steering is done with a shift of weight rather than a turning of the front wheel, aided by a phenomenon called "counter steering" that seems nonsensical until you've experienced it. Briefly put, counter steering enables the rider to initiate a turn by a combination of leaning into the turn while at the same time pointing the front wheel slightly to the outside of the curve. Sounds crazy, but that's how it is with two-wheeled conveyances.

The grade down into Cottonwood is so steep that I rarely pedal, but when I do, I'm cranking a big-front-ring-to-small-rear-sprocket ratio, all the while tucked into a full aero position, pedals level, chin a few inches from the handle bars. Whatever the Yarnell Grade took away from me, the exhilarating rush of speed and the beauty of motion through sun-warmed air has given it back. Near the bottom, I calculate that if I had to ride this 3,700 ft. of elevation *uphill*, it would take an hour-and-change, and burn 1,500 calories. In the direction I'm going, I'll have gone from the summit to the Verde River bridge in less than 30 minutes, and burned the caloric equivalent of an Oreo cookie.

In Cottonwood, Dur and I resume our rotation, and life is back to pick-and-shovel, workaday normal. Due to the narrow roads, the follow van is again forced to detour the touristy town of Sedona and won't re-join us until Flagstaff. I'm on the shift through downtown, and the series of stop lights and crowded intersections make for annoyingly slow going. As frustrating as the holdups are, the chance of incurring a 15-minute penalty for running a red light keep me strictly legal. While I'm stuck in traffic, a teenager on a Huffy rides alongside and paces me for 3 or 4 traffic-jammed blocks. He's a chatty kid in baggy cargo shorts and a Sex Pistols T-shirt, and he blushes when I complement him on the yellow flames hand-painted on his bike. In return, he wants to know where I got the totally awesome flashlight clipped to my handlebars. When he asks where I'm going, I answer I'm going up the road a ways. He asks how far, and I answer, "Probably more than a mile." He says he'd go with me but he's headed to his Bible study group. *"My girlfriend got me interested , so . ."* I tell him he's made a good choice, but I'm not sure if he thinks I mean it's a good choice joining the Bible study group, or for following his girlfriend's wishes. The way he grins, I suspect it's the girlfriend. He's too young to legally buy a drink, but he's already missing a couple of teeth.

The slow progress through traffic in Sedona gives me a chance to look for my beautiful, blue-eyed niece, Gwenn, who lives nearby. When she first heard about the RAAM, she thought maybe she and her family would set up lawn chairs somewhere along the route and watch the racers go by, kind of like spectators at a Fourth of July parade, cheering and waving flags. I knew just enough about the event to dissuade her, but I look for her along the roadside anyway, half hoping she didn't waste her Sunday afternoon, and half hoping to see her --- which I don't. The futility of Gwenn's generous impulse is confirmed by discouraging logistics. Forty-five solo riders started days before us, and the remaining 256 riders started with us, 500 miles ago. The first few hundred miles see some teams and soloists clumped together, but drafting is prohibited, so there's never a peloton as in the Tour de France Within 24 hours the disparity between starting times, and average speeds spread the racers thin, all of which conspires to make the world's toughest bicycle race the world's least accessible spectator event.

Highway 89-A winds northward out of Sedona along the southward-flowing waters of Oak Creek. The road has one lane in each direction and there are no shoulders. Traffic is heavy and I'm moving up through the Canyon so

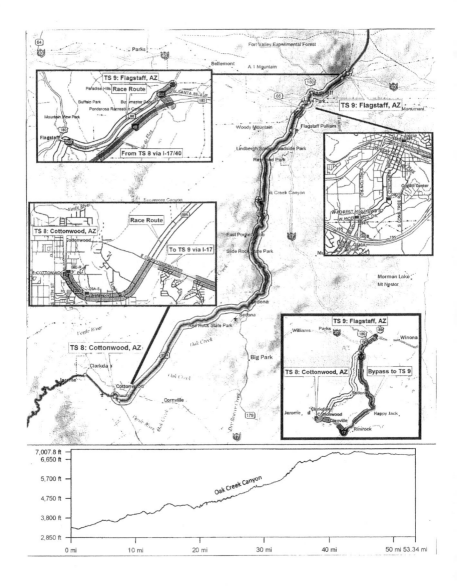

slowly that I *especially* don't dare risk riding in the travel lane. Hugging the fog line at the edge of the road often means getting whipped by roadside branches, but better to be stung by the bough of an aspen than crushed by the hood of an Escalade. Without the follow van trailing us, we have no protection in this section.

In the first 20 miles north of Sedona, Dur and I climb about 2,700 ft. up and out of Oak Creek Canyon. The pitch is only a fraction less steep than the Yarnell Grade, 128 feet of climbing per mile, and our pace through Sedona to time station # 9 in Flagstaff will turn out to be the slowest section -- a miserable 13.74 mph average -- of the entire race. The numbers are daunting. We surely won't break any records at this pace. Our exchanges are quick enough, but I can't tell how Dur is faring. I hope he feels better than I do. When one of us is on the road and the racer van leapfrogs past, it's impossible to gauge how fast the rider is going or how he's feeling. What I do know is that I'm riding badly. The hubris I indulged in on the other side of the mountain comes back to taunt me. *Ride without sleep like a soloist?* How naive of me. Hubris may be permissible as a young man's failing; at my age it's either impermissibly pitiful or a symptom of galloping senility.

From the RAAM route book

"Don't leave Flagstaff without enough good drinking water to last 275 miles to Time Station 14 in Cortez. Dangerous traffic is likely as you leave Flagstaff. High desert vegetation diminishes as the road drops and the brown, yellow, red, white and gray colors of the cliffs dominate the views. Many elk warning signs early in this section. At about mile 39, the race enters the jurisdiction of the Navajo Nation and clocks shift from Mountain Standard to Mountain Daylight Time. We will be guests

of various tribes almost all the way to Time Station 15 in Pagosa Springs, CO. Be respectful of their culture."

It's early evening when we cross Interstate 40 at Flagstaff. The last 15 miles have leveled out at 7,000 ft. and despite the altitude, my energy has returned, Dur apparently feels good, too, and we're finally making some respectable speed.

Racer van driver/navigator Nate Keck

"Finally, somewhere just past Flagstaff, AZ, I receive news that Dave has been released from the hospital and is recovered enough to rejoin the race in Tuba City. This means that the team will be back to full strength, and not a moment too soon. We'll all be relieved to see Dave race in a much more calculated manner and do his best for the rest of the event."

Dur is on the road a few miles behind us when we pull onto the shoulder to prepare for the exchange. As I get out of the van and unfold my left leg, I'm seized by an excruciating hamstring cramp. I'm not a chronic cramp-sufferer, as some cyclists are, but when I'm seized, there is nothing to do but suffer until it subsides, which can take up to 2 minutes of paralyzing pain. *If only Lydia were here!* A cramped hamstring can turn a limber leg into a fencepost. I've tried every trick known to cyclemankind and still haven't found a way to undo a hamstring cramp before *it* decides it wants to be undone. Dur has had a couple of near-cramping episodes, but none that blossomed into full paralysis mode, as this one has. Here in the evening sun outside Flagstaff, Arizona I can't walk a step, let alone get back on a bike until this agony is over. Holding onto the van door with white-knuckled despair, I gasp and groan enough to alarm Chris and Nate. But there's nothing anyone can do but wait it out and try to stretch it loose before Dur arrives.

Cramping is generally attributed to lack of fluids and electrolytes, but I've been religiously drinking gallons of water loaded with a balance of electrolytes, and my stomach has not once protested. Dur uses 2 bottles of Hammer HEED for the first two hours, then changes to Hammer Perpetuem for the rest of his shift. I use Ultragen's E.F.S. throughout the ride. Both our choices have always proved effective, as far as we can tell. (As a recovery drink, low-fat chocolate milk is claimed to be equally helpful as any sports brand, is cheaper and tastes much better!) But there's no guarantee that extreme muscle fatigue won't cause cramps despite an abundance of fluids and electrolytes. Lack of nutrition could also be a factor, but I've been eating prodigious proportions of everything Manny prepares for the racer van cooler: turkey-avocado wraps, fruits, potato chips and cookies. I'm certain fatigue is the culprit, but I'll never know. Before the RAAM is done there will be a few other phantoms of fatigue stalking me, but this evening's cramp will thankfully be the last.

I finally get on the bike without incident, wait for Dur to pull up to my wheel, and take off -- cautiously. The exchange is smooth enough, but for the next few miles I'm reluctant to push too hard. The slightest tightening of the hamstring could mean the cramp is returning, and cramping on the bike at high speeds is a messy proposition. Luckily, there are no further symptoms, and by the end of my pull I'm moving as if the incident never happened. The test remaining is the dismount from the bike and getting back into the van, but once I've successfully accomplished those maneuvers a few times, I resume riding hard. Aside from a 400-ft. bump 10 miles north of Flagstaff, most of the next 60 miles to Tuba City is downhill, a blessed reprieve. As the setting sun casts our shadows long and willowy off to our right side -- we're going due north again -- we become low-flying machines, redeeming the 90-minute crawl up Oak Creek Canyon with a comfortable average of 22.03 mph. Weary as I am, the speed feels great, even *deserved,* as if some inexplicable gesture of beneficence were randomly applied to our fanatical endeavor. We've lucked out with the right road at the right time. The cramps are gone and my mind is alert and re-settled into an interval of comfortable optimism. I want to believe that the RAAM bestows these little acts of divine intervention now and then upon its luckiest pilgrims, among whom I hope we are counted -- but then, who knows? There's always that next hill, that next challenge waiting and able to dope slap us back to reality.

Somewhere short of Tuba City, Dave Eldridge appears out of nowhere and loads me into his van. I'm so damned tired I can't pretend I'm not glad to see him, but I hate to be leaving my partner alone to finish off the shift to Tuba City. Dur may have slept even less than I did last night, and those final miles to Tuba City are going to hurt.

Dur Higgins

"That last, long, and very hot stretch from Flagstaff to Tuba City seemed like an eternity. I was getting very irritable with Nate Keck because I felt like he was not leveling with me when I would ask him, 'How much further?' It seemed he was under-reporting the actual mileage, thinking it would keep my spirits higher, but it worked to the contrary when I began to realize I was being gamed. How could we have 30 miles to go at the beginning of a 7-mile pull and still have 28 to go at the end of the pull? I think the stress and hard riding and heat were really getting to me -- probably to Nate, too, who I know was trying his best to keep me going. Adding to my irritation was the eye

infection I had contracted the night before while going by the stockyards. But the good news was that Dave Burnett and his bikes were being delivered to Tuba City, which was a relief to me on 2 levels: I was shot and needed sleep, and I was relieved to know Dave would be back in the saddle again, both figuratively and literally."

The team exchange in Tuba City takes place between highway 160 and a busy gas station/general store that sells everything from chainsaws to diapers. It's 10 o'clock at night, and the rows of fluorescent tubes in the huge canopy above the pumps cast a pallid version of daylight to the far corners of the pot-holed parking lot. It's a forlorn, dusty place with customers in crumpled pickup trucks and a skittish, skinny dog prowling the pavement for scraps. I see a few elderly women carrying sacks of groceries from the store, walking slowly away from the unbecoming light until they disappear into the darkness alongside the highway. As usual, our beleaguered crew is desperate for edible nourishment, and although I'm well fed, I'm still hungry enough to be tempted to look for some junk food calories in the store. As I'm about to open the door, I meet Barney Brannen coming out.

Barney introduced me to mountain biking 15 years ago, and we have been close friends ever since, sharing multiple cycling adventures around New England, the American West and Spain. When I signed up for the RAAM, Barney immediately volunteered to be part of the crew despite my concerns that his job might be more grueling than mine. He's often the first person I speak with at team exchanges, and I can always rely on him to know what's going on within the team, the crew and the world beyond. His willingness to make this cross country trip with me is a gift of generosity I'll never forget.

He looks sheepish when he sees me glance at the lump of a pre-packaged sandwich he's holding. "Mystery meat," he says. "I'm not sure what it is, but I'm counting on it to be awful enough to keep me awake for another 8 hours." I've seen Barney passed out dead asleep in the driver's seat of the RV, and I know he's exhausted while at the same time, inexhaustibly energetic. Whip-smart and a talented cyclist, kayaker, ice-and-rock-climber, hockey player, mountaineer and bon-vivant, Barney is always ready for the next adventure. But now, a second glance at the sad imitation of *food* he's holding makes me wonder if this adventure in Gas Station Cuisine might be one of the more dangerous of his career. He takes a bite of the awful thing, decides not to swallow and discards the remains in a trash barrel. When the skinny dog comes over, takes a few sniffs and keeps on walking, I decide to forego junk food and get ready for bed.

Howard Conway

"Early on in the race it became evident that finding a place to sleep was not easy, which is when I crawled in the big, rear bunk with Lewis and told him I had to sleep. Prior to that, we tried to sleep on the little side bunks but it was killing both of us. So we started sleeping together, first time I had ever slept with a man. Lewis is a real man's man, an officer in the Army who had been to 'Ganny' a few times -- that's short for Afghanistan. He could walk the walk and talk the talk, and he was a University of Tennessee football fan, and those are hard to find as we haven't been winning like we used to. So we bonded pretty quickly just on that. He was also working at a major bank so we had some other stuff in common. He told me some pretty crazy stuff about 'Ganny' and I know he has seen a lot in his tours over there. I will bet his men would have died for him, he

just seemed like that kind of leader. He was a great driving partner and sleeping buddy, and better at this surviving hardship stuff than me as I have grown soft since my days of being raised on a hilly old hardscrabble farm in WV, scratching out a supplemental living with my Dad as I was growing up.

The other thing I learned early on was that rider exchanges were messy, everyone was falling all over themselves, it was just a real cluster, wrong bikes on the racer van, wrong supplies, we should have practiced before the race. The riders were very little help, they just seemed unable to take care of themselves. When they got off the bikes they were like in a daze and didn't know what to do next, shit, shower, massage, eat, they had no idea, and understandably so as they were probably brain dead as well as body dead, suffering from fatigue, lack of sleep and amazingly 70+ years old. I hope I can remember my name when I am 70. I knew they were exhausted, and why wouldn't they be, but the lost-in-space wandering around got to be grating on the crew."

Prior to our arrival in Tuba City, crew chief Dave books a single hotel room for the racers and crew. He explains to the puzzled clerk that he needs the room for only a few hours, and he needs 19 towels. Most of the team gets in line and has their first -- and final -- RAAM shower inside a real bathroom until we get to Annapolis. I'm one of the last to enjoy this luxury, and when I leave the room, there's a puddle on the floor and a pile of wet towels 2 feet high.

Howard Conway
"There was a new hotel in Tuba City, a restaurant and gift shop all built by the Indians on the Reservation. I walked through the hotel and it was decorated in Indian items,

blankets and artifacts hung on the walls and the colors coordinated with American Indian colors. It was a beautiful hotel and they had built a Kiva in the side courtyard. I read a plaque about it. 'A subterranean kiva remained 50 degrees Fahrenheit all year round. So for the Ancestral Puebloans, it stayed cool in the summer, and only a small fire was needed to keep it warm in the winter'. *It had been really hot that day out in the middle of the hilly, rock strewn desert. I felt bad for the riders, but especially bad for the Indians. We had banned them to this awful area where nothing would grow. It's no wonder they resent us so much. While on the reservation we were told to be sure and behave. The Indian Police force is the law and they are especially hard on visitors. We were told last year several people ran into trouble for urinating on Indian land when no toilet was available. We were told not to take pictures of Indian possessions or people. Can't say I blame them. What an awful area to send them to."*

After a quick Tuba City massage by Lydia and a bowl of Manny's spaghetti and chicken, I am in my bunk with the covers over my head, as ready and needy for sleep as I have ever been. The section Dur and I just completed from Flagstaff, added to the 197 miles we rode the first night from Brawley to Salome, plus the 50-some miles we rode when we stepped in for Michael between Congress and Prescott, adds up to almost 400 miles covered in the last 24 hours -- on 2 hours of sleep. The overall team average, including the steep Yarnell Grade and Oak Creek Canyon and the 3-man segment of 266 miles, is still a surprising 18.72 mph. Team T430 is doing all right, and Dur and I are out cold before the RVs start rolling.

From Tuba City, Michael and Dave start off to the team exchange in Montezuma Creek, UT. The night air is cool and the roads are empty and fast. At time station # 11 in

Kayenta, AZ , Michael and Dave post an average speed of 21.44 mph since they left Tuba City. They've become the speed demons of darkness and are lucky as well. They have no way of knowing that the day before, a Canadian soloist, Jason "The Hammer" Lane, on his way through Kayenta, passed by the same right-hand turn on the same road they pass by tonight. Minding his own business, riding fast and feeling strong, Jason was hit by a car.

Soloist Jason Lane

"After 670+ miles, I was heading through Kayenta, AZ, about to head into Monument Valley, when a vehicle pulled up alongside, accelerated by me and without warning made a quick right turn just ahead. I was cruising downhill at a speed of 30+mph and had nowhere to go but into the car. With just enough time to grab my brakes, I managed to skid my back tire around, but I T-boned the side of the car with my left hip and arm. I came back to consciousness just in time to watch the rear tire run up and over my elbow. I could scarcely believe what was happening. Why are they still driving!? According to a bystander, after I fell to the ground, the vehicle briefly stopped, then began to drive away again with me lying half under the car. I was dragged a short distance and then the rear tire ran over my left shoulder blade and arm, as evidenced by the tire pattern printed both on my jersey and tattooed onto my back. How I managed to avoid my head being run over, I don't know. After about five hours of treatment in the ER, I was released with a few bandages and prescriptions, got on my back-up bike, and began limping my way into the evening sunset ride through Monument Valley. The events in Kayenta necessitated quite a bit of physiotherapy along the rest of the trip to deal with the injured left leg, but we still made it across in less than eleven days with no lasting injuries, nothing shy of a RAAM miracle."

Jason's story is unusual but inevitable in an event like the RAAM, where the aggregate exposure per racer-mile is enormous. Given the many thousands of hours that fatigued RAAM racers and support crews are on the road, it's a testimony to the event's strict safety protocols -- and luck -- that there are not more accidents like Jason's. For anyone who rides a bike on public thoroughfares, the only intelligent strategy for survival is to assume that every vehicle in sight is determined to kill you.

From Kayenta, AZ, Michael and Dave speed down Rt. 163 towards Mexican Hat, UT, pop 88, located on the Navajo Nation Indian Reservation. The tiny settlement is named after a nearby, prominent rock formation shaped like a sombrero, but it's hidden in darkness tonight.

Ken Gunnells

"As we entered Mexican Hat, UT, road signs warned of a dangerous, 90-degree turn at the bottom of a long, downhill pitch. Nate and I warned Dave about it, and off he went, down the hill at top speed with the follow vehicle's high beams shining the way. Anyone who hasn't been on a fast, "whippy" road bike may not know that they can actually corner faster than a car. Especially faster than the soft-sprung Dodge mini vans our team rented, and especially if the bike is ridden by an expert like Dave Burnett. Dave put the fear of smashed guardrails and deep ravine roll-overs in our minds as we tried to follow him. RAAM rules say you can't let the racer leave your headlights, but the widening gap between us was beyond our control. By the time Dave made it to the dangerous curve, Nate and I were screaming in anger (and a little fear). At great risk, we had stayed with him - but it seemed so reckless and so unnecessary so early in the race. The

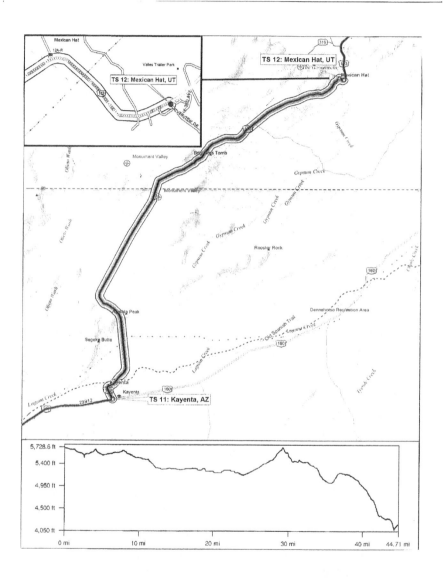

best/worst part? Dave underestimated the 90 degree turn, skidded his rear tire across the dusty pavement, did a classic, motocross, one-foot-down 'dab' and exited the corner in perfect form."

Dave's wild descents and bike handling are all a part of his personality, disconcerting as it is to the risk-adverse crew. But, aside from the risk-taking, tonight he is showing his best fast-lane stuff. Even the 1,000 ft climb between Mexican Hat and the team exchange in Montezuma Creek, UT, doesn't prevent him and Michael from posting an average of 18.42 mph. These numbers are more compelling than any physician's prognosis. Team United4Health is healthy and making good speed into the rising sun.

Dur and I are awake and eager to roll when Michael and Dave arrive at daybreak for the team exchange in Montezuma Creek. They rode 156 miles since Tuba City at an average of over 21 mph, bringing our overall accumulated average to 19.16 mph. We're on the edge of the Ute Mountain Indian Reservation at an elevation of 4,500 ft., and it looks like we're in for a beautiful day. Riding up onto the western slopes of the Colorado Rockies, cactus and sage brush have given way to conifers and aspen as the elevation increases and the soils hold more moisture.

The first 50 miles are disappointingly difficult, virtually all uphill, and it takes forever to climb 1,700 ft. to Cortez, CO, at elevation 6,190 ft. From Cortez, we climb another 2,000 ft. in the next 30 miles, but we seem to be slowly shaking off the fatigue that yesterday's efforts cost, and the big mountain scenery quickens our spirits as well as our pace.

Near the top of the 8,400-ft. pass west of Durango, CO, Taylor, Nate and I are anticipating Dur, who will appear in about 10 minutes. As usual, we've arranged the trade-off location on an uphill slope so that the slower speeds in and

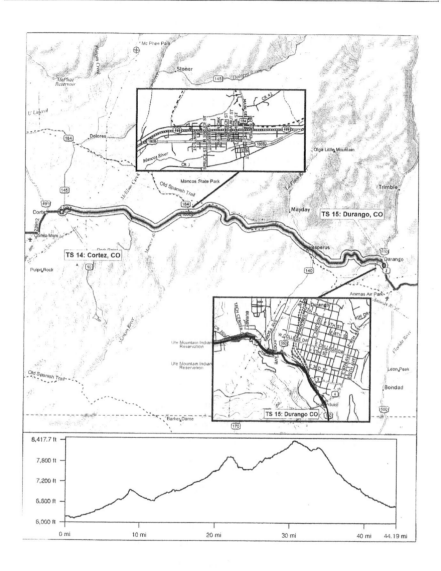

out of the exchange are less time- consuming. We are high on a mountainside with staggering views unfolding for miles in all directions. It's a warm, wildflower day under a perfect blue sky dotted with cotton-ball clouds, pure cycling heaven. As we're waiting, a Colorado Fish and Game warden stops across the road and jogs over to us. My immediate concern is that he has bad news for us about Michael or Dave.

The warden immediately puts us at ease. He's had a report of a road-killed bear, and he wants to know if we've seen it. He speculates it may have been picked up by a passing truck or dragged off the road by a Good Samaritan motorist. We've seen nothing, and I am humbled by the drab and commonplace nature of my recent road kill inventory. A squashed muskrat is nothing compared to a black bear. I also wonder what it would be like to encounter a bear at the downhill speeds we've been reaching. Several decades ago, a white-tail deer jumped out in front of my motorcycle in the New Hampshire woods. The unfortunate deer died quickly, while it took me 2 hours to drag myself out of the boondocks and into a hospital. A torn meniscus, cracked scapula and a medley of road rash eventually healed, but a fear of unannounced animals crossing the road never quite left me. I was traveling at only 35 mph and the Yamaha weighed 275 lbs. Hitting a 275 lb. bear at 50 mph on a 14-lb. bicycle is too grisly to contemplate. We assure the warden we'll call him if we see anything. The idea of another *ursus americanus* crossing my path on the 1,800-ft. plunge down into Durango ought to keep me alert all the way to the bottom.

Just after the game warden leaves us, we catch sight of Dur coming up the mountain about a mile-and-a-half away. It's near noon, with perfect visibility, and we can clearly see he is all alone on the wide, four-lane road. As usual, he is riding fast. One hundred yards below us is a thicket of aspen on a curve in the road. It's position in our sight line causes us to briefly lose sight of Dur. As we patiently watch for him to reappear, a white RV, plastered with RAAM race team decals, comes speeding up the grade. As it emerges on our side of the aspen grove, it abruptly stops, and backs down behind the trees to a point where we can no longer see it. We wonder what's going on. Moments later, a young rider in an orange jersey suddenly emerges from behind the trees. He looks improbably strong and fresh as he pedals by us and up over the summit. The white, reclusive RV with the RAAM decals follows immediately behind him.

In the 3,000 miles of the RAAM, our team sees perhaps a fifth of the 56 teams racing, and as various abilities are sorted out within the first few hundred miles, half of that fifth is never seen again. We've passed several riders, but the likelihood of passing or being passed by more than a few is rare. Teams inevitably fall into a cohort of 3 or 4, and barring misfortune, that's how it goes all the way to Annapolis. We get to know our fellow travelers; we cheer them on when we pass them, and are cheered on by them when they pass us. It's all very friendly and supportive, and by the time we're out for 2-3 days, we are a moveable family. Among our constant cohort all the way to Maryland is Team Bacchetta from Florida, three sun-tanned guys and a gorgeous blonde woman riding recumbents, all very friendly. As we learn later, they will set a new record for mixed recumbents in the under-50 age group. Their total elapsed time will be exactly 30 minutes faster than ours. We may have to flagellate ourselves at the post-race shrine of *Coulda, Woulda, Shoulda,* and geekily lament that 30 minutes at 19 mph translates to a measly 9.5 miles. We may also note that a 30-minute difference in total elapsed RAAM time amounts to a difference of .06 mph. *Ahhh,* if only, if only. . . And so it goes.

Our other reliable cohorts are the lively 8-person team,

Georgia Chain Gang, and the raucous Spirit of Brazil team, one of 5 from that country in this year's event. These midnight gauchos blare samba dance tunes through their follow-van's rooftop speakers from dusk until dawn. I love hearing samba beats competing with the endless drone of crickets when we're racing along a lonely, dark road. The Brazilians' mobile festival in late night RAAMland is wonderfully surreal, exactly the kind of cultural juxtaposition that helps offset the eternal tedium of pedal-left, pedal-right, repeat as required for 157 hours.

A few others teams will come and go, and we will begin to pass the slowest of the 47 soloists in Missouri, but the suspect in the orange jersey is categorically not in our cohort. We're 840 miles from Oceanside, and we've never seen his freshly-laundered ass or his RV before, and, most importantly, we *saw* he did not ride up from the bottom of the mountain. Taylor calls into race headquarters and reports what we've just not seen. They've already received two complaints about this guy and remind us there are over 20 race officials constantly travelling portions of the route watching out for infractions, which range from disregarding a stop sign to the rare instance of blatant cheating, such as we've just witnessed. Minor offenses, like ignoring a red light, can result in 15-minute team penalties. Serious transgressions mean removal from the race, but the number of these is miniscule. (We learn later that team Orange Jersey "retired" in Kansas.)

Dur comes in strong, we do a smooth transition at full speed and I take off. I have no reason to or likelihood of catching the cheater, but I start off too fast, caught up in a cyclist's version of road rage -- or, at least, road *anger.* This insult to meritocracy makes me unreasonably upset. The notion of cheating in an event like the RAAM baffles me. Why go to all the effort and expense of entering if you take the bus up the hill and coast down the other side? There's no prize money, no late-nights with David Letterman, no recognition at all beyond the tiny population aware of, or even caring about, the RAAM. The stakes are so low! The more I think about it, the faster I go down the grade to Durango, and the faster I go, the steeper the grade gets.

As if to remind me that this guy's impoverished stunt is not my problem, a nasty cross wind comes up off the valley floor and almost knocks me over. Wind is a wily saboteur of TT bike handling at 40 mph, its effect much more scary than bears across the road. I move my hands off the aero bars in front of me and out to the side bar ends, hoping for more leverage, more control, but the gusts are still moving me all over the pavement and my front wheel is determined to dance the speed wobble. This cyclists' version of Dirty Dancing develops when the front wheel begins to oscillate side to side and sets up a harmonic resonance in the frame. What begins as a troubling vibration can amplify to a widening, sideways sine curve, the worst case of which will require an ambulance. High speed spills are almost guaranteed to remove some skin from the hips, knees, shoulders and elbows. Even worse are broken collarbones, fractured pelvises and torn rotator cuffs. We hate it when that happens.

My first experience with speed wobble was during a cold and rainy downhill pitch on New Hampshire's Kancamagus Highway. What may have begun as cold-induced, involuntary shakes turned frightening within seconds. I was close to losing control of the bike when one of my riding companions, Joe Tonon, a former pro racer, told me to pinch the top tube of the frame with my knees and feather the rear brake until I slowed down below the wobble threshold. Here in these sunny Colorado Rocky Mountains, I repeat the lesson learned and finally bring the bike into a solid, straight line.

Coming down into the outskirts of Durango, the wind noise is at last out of my helmet, my adrenalin subsides, and I ease back into the aero bars, moving fast and smooth. When I'm slowed by traffic, I think about the bear and what it must have been like for it to have been struck by a two-ton vehicle. Did it have time to be scared, or was it *thump*, lights out? Was it doing what it loved to do just as we're doing what we love to do, if bears can be said to *love what they're doing?* Do bears cheat? I want to think they don't, because my unfounded bias classifies wild animals as somehow more honest and innocent, more gallant than we humans. But, hey, what am I thinking about bears for in the middle of the RAAM? Is the big toe on my right foot getting numb? Look at that tree! *Am I going A.D.D.?* I'm hungry and feeling grumpy about the dead bear and I'm disgusted with the cheater. I wonder what the terrain will be like for the next 80 miles. If I just came down 1,800 ft., how soon will we be going back up? What's that clicking noise? *Do I need some chain lube?*

A Stop sign ahead tells me to slow down, and the word "Stop" abruptly reminds me to *stop this cascade of random thoughts.* If I'm to ride the bike as fast and safely as I can, I need to concentrate on the road. My legs are only a bit uncomfortable, but I'm becoming mentally unreliable. This chaotic stream of free associations and non-sequiturs zipping in and out of my brain are sending signals I can't ignore. We've been on the road for only 2 days, but it appears I have entered a state of mind I'll hereafter identify as *RAAMbrain.*

The RAAM's most common medical problems, aside from the mental, are cramping, de-hydration, electrolyte depletion, saddle sores and the dreaded Shermer's neck. This cruel disorder is named after veteran soloist Michael Shermer whose exhausted neck and back muscles prohibited him from holding up his head during the 1983 RAAM. In the ensuing years, victims of Shermer's neck have devised imaginative, makeshift devices to replace the indisposed muscles. Some have come up with makeshift cervical collars and thick, foam chin supports which allow the afflicted rider to rest his/her head on the handlebars. Others cobble together random materials found alongside the road and Jerry-rig a mast extending up the spine for 1 or 2 feet above the helmet. Attached at the top of these Rube Goldberg masts might be makeshift chin straps devised to hold up the rider's 10-pound cranium; picture duct tape and a tree branch. It's doubtful that anyone goes into the RAAM with a Shermer's neck prosthesis in hand, but the fear of needing one is always present. Even with only 2 days of racing, we all have the beginnings of sore necks, but nothing like Shermer's so far. Except for Dave's early misfortune, a few painful cramps and an assortment of tolerable aches and pains that we septuagenarians deserve for our folly, we are all doing exceptionally well.

Our stint through Durango is followed by 50 miles of rolling terrain at an average elevation of 6,800 ft. Neither Dur nor I seem to mind the thinner air or the traces of smoke in our lungs from forest fires to the north. The forests here are green and majestic, the roads are smooth and we are making good speed until we come to a road construction project. A long line of traffic is stopped in front of us when we arrive, 30 or 40 vehicles with their engines turned off, as if the drivers know this will take a while. A few hundred yards ahead, we can see flag men standing in the lane with portable STOP/SLOW signs and earth-moving equipment loading boulders into trucks. Nate gets out of the van and jogs up to the front of the line to see if we can squeeze through. Dur is on his bike at the head of the line, waiting for a legal go-ahead. We've seen two other riders disappear up ahead and continue on through the construction zone, but Nate is strictly professional when it comes following RAAM rules and cautions Dur to wait. Five minutes later, Nate comes back shrugging his shoulders, *maybe yes, maybe no.* He stops at the third car in front of us. The occupant is a RAAM course official, possibly out here to check on the orange-jerseyed cheater. Nate had noticed the RAAM decals on the car when he jogged by to see about passing the flag man, and now he questions the official about the rules covering this roadblock situation. Could we proceed if the flag man allows it?

Every person we've met connected with the RAAM organization has been unfailingly polite and professional. This guy, alas, is neither. Instead of simply advising Nate to wait until all traffic is allowed to move, he emphasizes that he will be watching us like a hawk, and if we so much as pedal *one stroke* past our allotted position, we'll be penalized to the fullest. Polite as ever, Nate thanks him for the clarification and brings the news back to the van. We never know if the two riders who made it through were observed or penalized. What we know for sure is that Colorado's highway beautification program cost us 25 valuable minutes.

Lost minutes are part of the typical RAAM experience. Our delays can't be so different from everyone else's, although there will be moments when we'll inevitably think, *'If only there hadn't been. ..'* This road repair event will emerge as the longest delay we suffer, but on my shift alone, there were two others that resulted in another 15 or 20 minutes' deficit. The first was a similar road construction project, also in Colorado, which had, as an added bonus, a mile of freshly graded gravel. Riding 23 mm, tread-less tires pumped up to 120 psi on sharp, loose gravel makes me pucker up just to write about it. The opportunity for a puncture is extreme, the vibration shakes you silly, and

-- in the event that the pickup truck driver passing your shoulder holds an ingrained contempt for grown men wearing spandex -- the ability to track the bike exactly where you need it to be is marginal at best.

The second delay I encounter is at a freight train crossing. I'd read about crossings where RAAM riders were immobilized forever while a 200-car freight train rumbled by at an excruciating 7 mph. My train is neither quite so long nor quite so slow, but it does allow me a conversation with a retired physician, who gets out of his car to speak with me. Our brief exchange reveals that he is an avid cyclist who is considering the RAAM "someday". When he asks how it's going, I say it's going great. When he asks if I think *he* should try it, I look at his white hair and fit appearance and urge him to sign up for 2013. "There's an expiration date on bucket lists," I say. "Shelf life ain't what it used to be." This physician is the only civilian I encounter who knows anything about the race. He even knows someone on one of the teams entered. When the caboose comes by, we shake hands and I take off and try to make up for lost time.

Our average speed at the end of this 148-mile section with 5,500 ft. of climbing will be 17.23 mph. The road construction delay hurt the average badly, but calculating averages in the mountains can also be misleading. For instance, if a rider averages 10 mph up a 10-mile hill and 30 mph down the other side of the same 10-mile hill, those mph numbers do not add up to a 20 mph average, as one might think. Since the hill took an hour to climb and 20 minutes to descend, those 20 cumulative miles take 1 hour and 20 minutes, so that the average speed over the up-and-down, 20-mile distance is only 15 mph. As long as it takes an hour to climb to the top of the hill, the speeds reached going down the other side don't help the average as much as we'd wish. Even if the rider was going *60 mph* down the hill, the average speed would still be only a little over 17 mph.

We've been on the road for two full days now, and the unnatural division of a day into thirds changes the typical sleep-at-night pattern into a sleep-when-you-can imperative. Among our many pre-race deliberations, the team discussed methods of getting to sleep, especially the deep, R.E.M. sleep needed to restore a fatigued body. While we all knew that skewed schedules and noisy, uncomfortable conditions would make sleeping especially difficult, our approach to the solution was split between the naturalists/purists, Michael, Dave and Dur, and the agnostic/pragmatist: me. The naturalists were determined to avoid prescription pharmaceuticals and stick with melatonin and other herbal products with which they'd had some success. I might add that Michael, Dave and Dur are exceptionally health-conscious. I'd be surprised if a Twinkie has ever passed their lips. I'm not so well-disciplined, but I have earnestly tried every natural and over-the-counter sleeping aid available and found nothing reliable. What's worse, I'm a sissy-light sleeper, can't help it. Buzzing flies wake me up and ticking clocks *keep* me awake. It was clear from the start that the RAAM's chaotic schedule and physical challenges would be impossible without adequate sleep. So when I told my team mates that my doctor had recommended Ambien, I might as well have confessed I was a crack addict. Stories of the drug's side effects are as colorful and frightening as they are statistically irrelevant, to *me,* at least. My search of the internet showed that, of the 13 *billion* doses used to date, the incidence of psychotic episodes, sleepwalking into the pool, driving the car to Burger King or painting the kitchen purple while asleep, is miniscule. When I returned from 2 weeks of intensive March training in Mallorca, I explained to my team mates how I took a 10 mg pill every night, slept like a baby and awoke refreshed. They were transparently dismayed by my fall from grace, so I stopped proselytizing and hoped their approach would be as successful as mine. To make sure there would be no surprises, I continued the experiment with Ambien until June, and the results continued to be 100% consistent and favorable. During the RAAM, I used it for every sleep cycle, and wouldn't have survived without it. When Lydia looked as if she was about to drop from exhaustion, I slipped her a pill, and it worked for her just as it did for me. Twenty minutes before I wanted to fall asleep, I would pop a pill, finish eating, brush my teeth, climb up into the bunk above the cab, clamp my padded Bose noise suppressors over my ears and slide into my sleeping bag. The crew could be talking, slamming doors, the RV bouncing over potholes -- flies buzzing, clocks ticking -- and yet within minutes I'd be dead to the world. Ambien's best feature was the jump start into deep, REM sleep, which then lasted for 3 + hours. With few exceptions, I slept about 4 hours during every recovery shift. Over a 48-hr period, that meant an average of 6 hours per 24, not a lot of sleep considering we were each racing an average of about 114 miles every 24 hours, but apparently (almost) enough for me. My health-conscious team mates may have slept less than I, but they never stopped riding like champions.

Around 2 p.m., Dur and I make it to the team exchange at an abandoned gas station in Pagosa Springs, CO. We are content with our day's work, but Dur's eyes are now alarmingly red-rimmed and uncomfortable; they look as if they are about to bleed. He consults with nurse Janice, and she suggests the redness is probably caused by the stockyard in California, the forest fire smoke we went through and the hot, dry climate. I sense that Dur worries it's more than that. He's told me he had an eye infection before, after riding in Florida.

Back then, he needed strong anti-biotics and was left with an "opacity" in one eye, so this isn't new to him. But he stays calm and lets Janice do a thorough examination. When she's finished, she excuses herself from the RV and confers with crew chief Dave near the open door. From what I overhear, the discussion is not so much about Dur's specific ailment, which Janice thinks is a minor irritation, but about how to keep his situation confidential and how to best manage his anxiety. A deliberate decision is being made with team morale in mind, and as long as the medical diagnosis is correct and Dur's eyesight is not in danger, it seems a wise one. When Janice comes back in the RV with eye drops, she downplays the possibilities of complications and assures Dur he's going to be all right within 24 hours. The additional good news is that the regularly updated RAAM website shows our team's average at Pagosa Springs' time station #16 is 18.8 mph at 912 miles into the race. If we compare the average mph set by the 2004 the Grand PAC Masters' team, whose record we aspire to beat, we would be about 125 miles ahead of where they were at this point in the race.

The sun won't set for another 6 hours, but Dur and I are asleep while Michael and Dave begin the epic pull up to Wolf Creek Pass and the Continental Divide, the quintessential climb of our western mountain odyssey.

"If you live long enough, the venerability factor creeps in; you get accused of things you never did and praised for virtues you never had."

I.F. Stone

DAY THREE
Pagosa Springs, CO to Ford, KS
503 miles

Dave Burnett

"Once back in the rotation, the thrill of racing eastward once again overwhelmed me. My teammates had successfully bridged my period of incapacity and I felt great. In fact, I might have felt better than they did because of my recovery/rest time while they were at work. The ride Michael and I did from Tuba City to Montezuma Creek convinced me I was strong again, but now I got in touch with a goal that I had set for myself before the race began. I knew that I would be doing much of the work when we climbed Wolf Creek Pass at the Continental Divide in Colorado. I had been sleeping in an altitude tent at altitudes as high as 13,000 ft and was prepared to deal with the 10,858 - ft elevation at the pass. In addition, my body just happens to climb well. I had calculated that our most conservative schedule would put us at the top of Wolf Creek Pass at 10:00 PM if we were on schedule to meet our goal and break the existing 70+ team record. My thinking was to set a goal for myself to have sun on my back as I crested the top, which would put us a quite few hours ahead of schedule. It was mid-afternoon as we approached the steep part of the pass -- nearly 10 miles at 6-8% -- and it became clearer to me just how well we were doing. Michael and I felt good. The climbing got steeper and I took increasingly long pulls, ready and thrilled to do the work. There were several other riders in our vicinity, and they provided great incentives for me to go faster. One such rider was a Stephen from Australia. We talked briefly and rejoiced in the occasion. Soon, a camera

crew from RAAM came along and started to film me. They asked how I felt and I remember saying to them, 'We're going to SMASH that frigging record!' We crossed the top somewhere around 3:30 in the afternoon. I not only had sun on my back, I had full sunlight."

East of the Continental Divide, all waters flow to the Gulf of Mexico or to the Atlantic Ocean. Crossing the Divide means the worst of the western mountains are behind us and we are nearing completion of the first third of the race. After cresting the 10,856 ft summit at Wolf Creek Pass, Michael and Dave ride several miles at over 2 miles high, speeding through forests of spindly spruce and gray patches of last winter's snow. They put on their wind jackets for the fast, cool downhill run through a pair of tunnels and down around wide, sweeping turns. Their labors up the western slopes are amply rewarded with a 4,600 ft. descent over the next 115 miles, a long, fast ride down the mountains on smooth pavement. Their average speed of 22.57 mph on the 153-mile pull to La Veta, CO is nothing short of spectacular. When they pull into La Veta , the team average at time station # 19 rises from 18.8 to 19.2 mph! Forget about graying hair: these guys are rock stars.

In the hour-long wait before changing places with Michael and Dave in La Veta, I take a short walk and think about why I'm loving this cross country lunacy, what it is that makes all of this even marginally appealing, the months of training, sacrifices, fatigue and danger -- the unrelenting nature of it all. The easy answer is that this is the level at which I need to live some of my life some of the time, not all of it all of the time, but enough to be energized by the deepest breath, to be challenged by the boldest risk. I'm cursed, or blessed, well, *stuck*, anyway, with having been born a high-energy, high metabolism, restless mammal. I

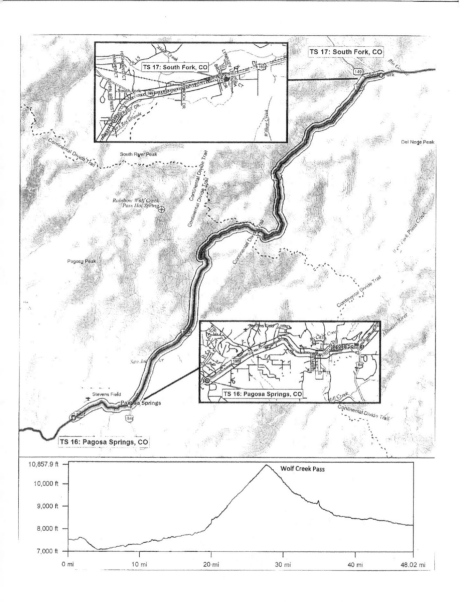

need to move a lot; I can't help it. I'm happy to sit and read and play with my granddaughters for an afternoon or evening, but I get itchy if I stay in one place indoors for too long. Intense, physical challenges expand my sense of control and make me feel I can succeed at anything I'm willing to work for. Physiologically, we know that a rise in heart rate and the accompanying surge of glucose, cortisol and adrenaline sharpens and focuses the mind; it puts me into a stimulating state of alert relaxation. For me, the RAAM's appeal is more about an adventure into the unknown than about a week of racing. I'm not so interested in racing others; what I'm drawn to is racing against (an idea of) myself, against the nature of predictability, and lately, I suppose, against age itself.

The question of why we are drawn to extreme activities has been pondered for millennia, but the answer is never quite satisfying. Why do people climb the Himalayas when there are plenty of lesser mountains? The routine answer, *"Because it's there"* is obvious, but incomplete. Why do we hunt, despite having plenty to eat? *"Hunting is an inherent trait."* Why do we labor anonymously for years on a novel, or commit to composing difficult music or visual arts that are never seen by the public? *"It's something I have to do."* Sigmund Freud aside, have there ever been adequately convincing answers to why we do the odd and difficult things we choose to do?

Barney Brannen

"In December 2010, Don crashed hard on his mountain bike. He was showing off to a pretty woman at the time. It wasn't his first mountain bike crash (or the first time he crashed his bike while showing off to a pretty woman), but this one was serious enough to inflict the final, intolerable insult to his long-abused shoulder, requiring major surgical

repair, in February of 2011, to all four muscles in his right rotator cuff. In October of 2011, just before serious training for the RAAM began, he had the other, long-abused shoulder repaired as well, and the resulting period of disability during the winter of 2011 threw him into an existential tailspin. I suppose we all must think from time to time how our lives might be affected by a disabling injury or, even, the inevitable physical deterioration of the aging process, but for Don, his physicality was an essential part of who he was. At 71, he appeared to have been affected less by the aging process than most of his regular riding buddies, all of whom were at least 20 years younger, but the sudden setback precipitated by his shoulder surgeries left him in a deep funk. He soldiered through the surgery and rehab with his usual, cheerful optimism – in fact, just six weeks post-surgery, he was (against all medical advice) back on a bike, riding in Mallorca, albeit gingerly – but it was clear he wasn't really back to normal. Though he never said as much to me, I sensed the whole episode forced him to look over the edge, into the abyss, asking himself if his body wouldn't allow him to do the things he'd always done – ride bikes with abandon, cut trails through the forest, or build stone walls in his gardens – who is he to become? Maybe the main reason Don accepted Michael Patterson's invitation to join the RAAM team was to conquer those demons, or at least stuff them back in the mental closet for a while."

My shoulder problems during the year before the 2012 RAAM were not unique. In an unnecessary show of solidarity, Michael crashed his TT bike in June of 2011. A few weeks later, his surgeon was pleased to see the broken collarbone was healing perfectly, but Michael still needed surgery to have a torn rotator cuff re-attached. He spent much of the summer with the same re-hab drills I knew too well, a slow process we both endured without much enthusiasm. Worse yet, in January of 2012, well into the beginning of his RAAM training, Michael was hit by a motorist in Florida and suffered a leg injury which kept him off the bike for several weeks. Elena and Melinda may have shared confidences about which husband grumbled most, but neither Michael nor I have been eager to hear their account of those difficult days.

Ten days before the RAAM began, I attended my 50th college class reunion. The usual suspects predominated, confident, accomplished men with illustrious careers, svelte trophy wives and tennis tans. Here and there among the grandees were also the sad remnants of former heroes, a wheelchair-bound fullback assisted by a nurse, a shining track star shuffling along on a walker. Missing altogether were 145 classmates -- 15% of our freshman class -- dead from causes typical of our demographic: cardio-vascular disease, cancer, traffic fatalities and 4 lives lost to war.

When I shared my excitement about the upcoming RAAM, the most common response was concern for my safety. I could get run over and killed. I could have a heart attack. I was crazy at "our age" to attempt such a grueling trek. When I thought about my 145 deceased classmates, I couldn't help but imagine they would give anything to scramble out of their graves and take the risk I'm taking, if only for a day. Is a life lived pumping the brakes worth the illusion of safety when it's randomly ambushed at 50? Life is a crapshoot in so many ways that I'm drawn to conclude that the older we get, the more "caution" is an over-rated commodity. The irony of matching age to danger is that the young, with so much life ahead of them, and with so much to lose, are far more likely to risk injury and death than their elders, who have relatively little life ahead of them, and relatively little to lose if the risk turns out badly.

The reunion was instructive, and many of the lives I saw unfolded were inspiring, but I was also aware that I will never be part of the archetypical senior's shuffleboard mind-set, can't imagine myself in a retirement village wearing sansabelt slacks and a cream-colored cardigan.

Changing attitudes about aging have ushered in a new demographic of older, elite athletes. Competitive cyclists, for instance, have achieved levels of performance in the 50 and 60-year-old categories that were previously thought unattainable. Just a decade ago, many race venues had no age categories beyond age 60. Now, age categories include 65, 70, 75 and even older groups for both women and men. As the population of 40 and 50-year-old athletes "age up", the numbers of racers in these older age brackets will increase dramatically, as will the quality of the performances.

There are several times during the RAAM when I think the town we're passing through would be an especially nice place to visit or even possibly live; La Veta, Colorado is one of them. Nestled in a valley beneath 10,000 ft. peaks, this little town has a friendly feel to it with older, single-story bungalows stretched out comfortably along wide, informal avenues. Our dusty caravan is parked next to an historic stone building in a modest, residential neighborhood. A pair of mule deer wanders close by, browsing the street-side shrubs, unconcerned with our presence. The crew seems to like La Veta as much as I do. This is our 7th team exchange, and the routine of setting up camp has become smooth and familiar. I am increasingly attuned to the crew's mood, and today the vibe seems conflicted. Every time we racers get back into camp, we're solicitously greeted with questions about how we're faring, how was it out there, do we need anything? But it's now obvious they're suffering from the relentless pace and lack of sleep just as we racers are. Seeing the growing fatigue on the crew's faces, I ask how they are doing before they get a chance to ask me. Ever professional, they project an upbeat attitude and spare me the details of their daily difficulties, but I wonder what the real story is, how all these people are coping with the many challenges among them.

Classic disaster stories from past RAAM expeditions include burning vehicles, blown transmissions, communication failures, long, wrong turns off the course, team mutinies, a hospitalization to remove a spider that crawled into a sleeping crew member's ear, and a few years ago, the unspeakable tale of a racer who relieved himself in the dark roadside woods, stepped in his fragrant creation and tracked it back into the van -- which had no AC during the hottest RAAM summer in years. This year's RAAM first near-disaster occurred a couple of days before the start, when Patrick Seeley's race bike was stolen. As he rushed to have a replacement built, one of his crew spotted the stolen bike, now painted *pink*, and brought it back to Patrick, who, along with his partner, went on to win the 2-person division. While Patrick's incident occurred even before the race began, once the RAAM takes to the road, the opportunities for mishaps become exponential. Just imagine the amount of *stuff* involved. It's inevitable that someone, somewhere in 3,000 miles will leave behind a pair of glasses, a cell phone, a camera, hat, jacket, or toothbrush, etc. With a crew of 15, leaving behind a crew member would be easy.

Barney Brannen

"After crossing the continental divide at Wolf Creek Pass, we barreled into eastern Colorado through cross winds so strong an occasional gust would blow the RV eight to ten feet sideways before I could pull it back into

our lane. With the Rockies behind us, we weren't quite halfway across the country, but the team had unmistakably overcome a major physical and psychological hurdle, only to encounter the next: exhaustion. The adrenaline we had relied on for the first couple of days and nights was completely depleted, and the combined effects of sleeplessness and a gas station diet were kicking in. The raw, ugly side of humanity was bubbling just beneath the rapidly fraying surface of our 'civilized' selves.

Imagine the pleasant surprise we encountered when we turned off the main road and rolled into La Veta, Colorado, an improbably quaint, artsy community, nestled in green, rolling hills, seemingly in the middle of nowhere. As we reckoned ourselves at least an hour and a half ahead of Michael and Dave, we parked the RVs in a shady spot on a back street, left Don & Dur to snooze a bit more before starting their shift on the bikes, and strolled over to eat a real, sit-down dinner at the La Veta Inn, looking out over the town green, dappled in early evening light filtering through the trees that surround the main square.

Unfortunately, it turned out we had underestimated the speed at which our racers were burning up the road, and a pleasant, almost 'normal' meal ended with rushed requests for boxes to go, as we hustled back to the RVs to get Don & Dur stirring, so they could dress and be fed comfortably in advance of the next team exchange. Still, it was a rare, restful moment, and certainly one of the only times (so far, THE only time) we actually sat down in a restaurant to eat a meal, rather than stuffing down in the cab of the RV the unspeakable (and unpronounceable) ingredients of pre-packaged, infinite shelf life delights dispensed in America's convenience stores.

As we were waiting for the incoming racers to arrive, I took the utility van and drove to the edge of La Veta to scout the route out of town, so we could give Don clear directions to get himself back en route without a missed turn. Leaving La Veta to the south, the racers would encounter a stiff climb up and over Cucharra Pass into vast, unpopulated lands before descending to Trinidad, Colorado, where we would cross I-25 and resume our eastward trajectory. At the edge of La Veta, maybe three-quarters of a mile from our camp, I noticed a convenience store and thought this would be a good place to grab a cup of caffeine (believe me, I had no expectation it would taste like coffee) on our way out of town."

From the RAAM route book

"Cuchara Pass is arguably the prettiest of the major Colorado passes. Narrower and curvier than the others (i.e. fewer team exchange spots) and noticeably quieter. Then after a 4,000 foot descent, you're "rewarded" with congested historic Trinidad streets.. . Check fuel, water and provisions in Trinidad! Very limited services on the route for the next 200 miles)."

Leaving La Veta at around 9 p.m., Dur and I start our rotation into a cool, stiff wind. We climb slow and hard over the first 17 miles, from 7,000 ft. up and over the Cuchara Pass at an elevation of 9,900 ft. It's cold at these heights at night, and this is the only occasion in 3,000 miles that I wear tights and an insulated wind breaker. The hours our team spent back in February agonizing over what special clothing to pack have far exceeded the time we spend wearing the items we so pathologically chose, but tonight I'm glad we made the fuss. Clothing aside, our efforts up and over the pitch-black pass keep us warm, but our hard work will extend through the next 45 miles into Trinidad, CO.

Barney Brannen

"After pushing Don off into the gathering dusk of a nearly-solstice sunset, we turned our attention to getting Michael and Dave through their post-ride ritual. In Dave Eldridge's carefully mapped-out plan, we were to have incoming racers showered, massaged, fed, bedded and rolling out of town within an hour of their arrival. The point was to get to the next exchange as quickly as possible so we'd all have at least a few hours to sleep in an RV that wasn't rocking and bucking its way across America's secondary roads. Lying in the designated "bedroom" of the RV, which, cantilevered far behind the rear axle, was likened to sleeping on a busy diving board ... so unpleasant in a moving vehicle that only Dur found it bearable, and that bedroom became his domain while Don, Dave and Michael slept either over the cab or on a fold-out sofa directly behind the cab.

By the team exchange in La Veta, we were lapsing into a pace Dave Eldridge considered too sluggish, mainly because the two guys who had just traded shifts riding bicycles very fast for eight hours were not inclined to rush through anything. On this evening in La Veta, Dave remonstrated with Michael Scholl and me to speed up the process, push the racers along and get us rolling out of town within the specified hour.

Ah, yes. 'Push the racers along' sounds so simple, doesn't it? Not surprisingly, grown men do not necessarily take kindly to being told what to do, even if they might, in an otherwise rational state of mind, objectively understand that it's in their own best interests. But men who have been racing bikes for three days and nights are not prone to be in "an otherwise rational state of mind," and some men, maybe the kind who indulge the fantasy of breaking a record for fastest time riding a bike across the continent, are probably less inclined toward rationality anyway. In fact, among the crew, we had raised quite a number of children, so we weren't without the benefit of prior experience when we began to assign some of our racers (I won't say which ones) maturity levels ranging on the narrow spectrum between 'dependent infant' and 'defiant toddler.'

Unfortunately, the hurry-up part of the process inevitably fell upon the meal portion of our racers' time in camp since that was the last activity to be accomplished before we could roll. Of course it was understandable that they did not want to be rushed while taking their well-earned sustenance (and, given the winding roads we were driving on most of the time, eating while in motion simply wasn't a viable option). Still, Michael Patterson and Dave Burnett were being particularly intransigent on this evening, and appeared irritated at Michael Scholl and me for being pushy. The rising levels of frustration among us quickly became palpable, until Dave Burnett brought the situation to a near boil by pointing an accusatory finger at me and declaring, 'Barney, I'm beginning to feel just like I did before I got sick the other night, and if you keep pushing me like this, I'm afraid I'm going to be sick again.'

I obviously wasn't pushing him for my own pleasure or sense of authority. In fact, I wasn't pushing him for any reason other than for his own good, which people more experienced and rational than he or I had long ago determined meant prioritizing sleep over eating at a drawn out, leisurely pace. And no one, not one of us, believed for a second that Dave's illness of two nights before had been precipitated by his inability to eat a leisurely meal relaxed in a chair."

Howard Conway

"Back in Parker, AZ, when Dave got sick, everyone felt sorry, but not so much for him as for the other 3 guys who eagerly picked up the slack and hardly lost a beat without

him. *When Dave came back in Tuba City, he was still a difficult person, but it reached a boiling point in La Veta. After the rider exchange that night, Dave B and Michael were showered and massaged and put in the Racer RV and Manny was serving dinner. Every time at a racer exchange, the following 4 things had to happen as fast as possible: shower, massage, food and cleanup. The RV's have got to get on the road and race to the next exchange point as fast as possible so we can stop the RV's from rocking, park and get some sleep. But not this night. Dave B would not eat right now, said he couldn't, and wouldn't let us drive on because if/when he wanted to eat, he couldn't while the RV was rocking. Every person in the crew was affected by this behavior. We couldn't go, had to wait and fix his meal when Dave was good and ready. As far as the crew was concerned, it was just a terrible action on his part. Discussions were rampant among the crew and everyone was pissed. Night was coming, we all needed sleep and we needed to get on the road. Finally, Lewis and I told Manny to take his food over to the racer RV and wait. A couple of crew members from the racer RV were so frustrated they moved over to ours, and we drove off, leaving the few remaining sitting around waiting for Dave B to eat."*

Barney Brannen

"Seeing that nothing good (and potentially something very bad) would come of prolonging this unfortunate situation, I advised Michael Scholl I would be taking a little stroll to the edge of town and buy us a couple of cups of coffee for the next leg of driving. He could pick me up on his way out of town, after the prima donnas had dined to their satisfaction and would condescend to be transported.

Walking out of La Veta, I was reminded how quickly and totally small towns without street lights get dark when the sun goes down and the population goes to bed. With no light pollution from buildings and streets, the night sky can become a dazzling show of stars. But on this night, a strong westerly wind was bringing in a cover of clouds that obscured the sky. Also, it hadn't occurred to me before I took my leave of the tensionfest at the RV that convenience stores in small towns don't stay open all night, and, in fact, the store I'd seen earlier was closed, its lights were off and the street was pitch black. Now I wondered if Michael might not see me as he rounded the corner at the edge of town, so I pulled out my cell phone to alert him to the unforeseen change in circumstances.

Across most of sub-Saharan Africa, people who live in grinding poverty carry cell phones and use them every day to communicate seamlessly with friends, colleagues and family members. I've seen Maasai herders, alone with their goats on the endless expanses of prairie near the Serengeti, wearing tribal garb that hasn't changed in centuries, chatting amiably on their cell as if it were the most natural (and reliable) thing in the world. A friend who works for the World Wildlife Fund once called me from the middle of the Kalahari desert. But in the United States of America, if you get more than a few miles outside of a 'Standard Metropolitan Statistical Area,' cell phone coverage becomes a hit or miss proposition.

And so it was in La Veta that night. I had just enough signal to connect with Michael but not enough to carry on a conversation. During our third attempt, I was standing by the side of the lonely road, waiving my arms and yelling into my useless cell phone as Michael drove heedlessly by. I assumed he would quickly realize that he had gone by the convenience store, since the town ends so abruptly and becomes wooded countryside, but I began to feel alarmed when the RV made a sharp left hand turn about a quarter mile up the road and I watched its tail lights disappear up the winding route to Cucharra Pass. When Michael didn't return in the next few minutes, I assumed he was so sleep-deprived that he had simply forgotten I was not on board. How far might he go before he came to the realization that he had left his co-driver behind? And since our vehicle was the last to leave camp, if Michael Scholl didn't pick me up, who would?

This might have seemed like a ridiculously implausible scenario if we hadn't heard from Dave Eldridge and others about crew members accidentally left behind on prior RAAMs. When you think about the effects of extreme sleep deprivation, it's kind of amazing that it doesn't happen all the time! Regardless, I was not enthusiastic about the prospect of becoming this year's left-behind poster boy.

After repeated, unsuccessful attempts to reach Michael over the next ten minutes (maybe it was only five minutes, but it seemed like thirty), we finally connected. He seemed surprised that he had not yet come upon the convenience store. (How far did he think I walked?) In any event, I assured him (in probably somewhat less than reassuring tones) that he was well on his way to Annapolis and that, if he wanted any future relief behind the wheel, he would need to return to La Veta to pick me up. Ten (or was it five) minutes later, the RV rolled up, I climbed in the navigator's seat in frosty silence, and Michael sheepishly apologized for his 'oversight'. But there was more: As a coda to our two-ships-passing-in-the-night comedy, Michael made a multi-point turnaround on the narrow road and rammed our rear-mounted bike rack into an embankment. As it turned out, there was little damage done to the rack and thankfully none to the $20,000 worth of bikes it carried. The only real setback was the *lost sleeping time (for racers and drivers) at the next team exchange, and it was for only a portion of that we could blame on ourselves."*

Michael Scholl

"I'm 65 years old and I've been a crew member on 6 RAAM teams. I was also on Dave Eldridge's crew for the 'Run Across America' which was very similar to RAAM except considerably longer in duration. I am an Information Security Manager for the State of Florida, and I decided to be a crew member for this 2012 team for the vicarious thrill of accomplishing something very big with riders who are even older than I am.

No stranger to discomfort, I endured Navy boot camp in 1967. When one of us made a mistake, all of us were made to pay for it in excruciating pain (like holding our rifles straight-armed out in front of us for 10 minutes). Preparing for this RAAM was a bitter-sweet memory of the military.

Once the pre-race jitters are over, the boredom and monotony of driving sets in. We consume heavily caffeinated beverages and talk and consume more caffeine and talk some more. When we arrive at an exchange point, we do our basic prep for the exchange and then we try to sleep, hoping to overcome the caffeine. Working under this stress in tight quarters is difficult. One of the best things that can pull a crew member through is to have a good partner. I was lucky to have Barney Brannen who was always up for some lively discussions. Our incessant chatter may have been an annoyance to some of the riders, but it helped to keep me awake and educated me on innumerable topics.

Having participated in multiple other RAAMs in support of 'professional' riders, I can draw a clear distinction from this experience. In the other RAAMs, the riders could often become petulant or cranky because a favorite food was unavailable or because someone didn't do something that they felt was necessary. Most of Team U4H seldom grumbled or complained except for remarks about soreness or stiffness from the brutal ride, which seemed reasonable enough."

Howard Conway

"I think some of the crew, especially the women, didn't realize this was a contest, a game, and we needed to play it better. I had been in and around a lot of football and basketball teams, played, coached, and managed leagues, so I tried to convince everyone this was just a big game and we needed to play it exceptionally well as a team if we were going to win. We would have to put all our hurt feelings behind us and work/sacrifice for the good of the team. Now don't get me wrong, for a lot of crew members, this was not their first rodeo, and they knew what was going on and what they needed to do, but there were some who had built-in resentments. Some of them thought the riders were flat out wealthy men. Right or wrong, they'd heard they were going to sponsor this whole trip on their own unless they found a sponsor. I don't know if that was true, or if it even mattered, but that was what some believed and resented. And when we read their bios we knew them to be extremely successful men. Probably not used to working with people as low in station as some of the crew, maybe early in their careers, but they were mostly executive/ professional types. It was an opinion that weighed out plus and minus as the race progressed and the tension reached its highs."

The RAAM's 31-year history has a solid safety record. Many riders are forced to drop out due to fatigue or injuries, but such is the nature of the world's toughest bicycle race. The only fatality in all those years occurred in 2005, halfway between La Veta and Trinidad. Bob Breedlove, a 53-year-old orthopedic surgeon was on his 5th RAAM when he collided head-on with a pickup truck. Whether he fell asleep or accidentally swerved across the road into the pickup, or the pickup swerved across the road and hit him, is a matter of dispute. Whatever the cause, the results were tragic. I learned about this grisly incident from watching a film about the RAAM in the first few weeks after signing on. Unfortunately, my wife Melinda also saw the film. She's also recently read that the incidence of cyclists' fatalities caused by motorists rose 8.7 per cent from 2010 to 2011. As wonderfully supportive as she is of my many adventures, Breedlove's death became emblematic of the reasons I should not enter the RAAM. Her concern touched me; being cared for is no small gift. But I was determined to go, and the best I could do was to promise to be safe -- as if I could guarantee such a thing -- but I meant to keep my word.

Now, her anxiety haunts me as we start down from the Cucharra Pass. What if her worries are warranted? I find myself wide-eyed at every turn and stay well within the lights of the follow vehicle. There have been times on a straight, dippy road, when going over the crest of a hill has left me in darkness for a few moments until the follow van's lights top the hill. I can ordinarily trust the road will be as straight as it's been for the last few miles even if I can't exactly see it for a few seconds, but tonight I am determined to stay well illuminated at all times. There's little traffic in this spooky stretch, but every oncoming vehicle reminds me of Bob Breedlove and my pledge to be careful. I can't help but think that somewhere in this section is that tainted ground where the thing that should never have happened did. I'm not sure whether it's better to know the exact location or let the indefinite keep me cautious.

We roll into mile-high Trinidad, CO, at an average below 16 mph. La Cucharra Pass was tougher than I imagined, but its difficulty probably had as much to do with residual fatigue from the days before as the climb itself, and I feel stronger now that we're down out of the cold, high mountains. Trinidad is one of Colorado's prettiest mile-high towns, or so we'll learn well after our 3 a.m. rush past the wealth of Victorian architecture spread out along dark, empty streets. Aside from a colorful history as a frontier mining town full of saloons and gunslingers, once presided over by Bat Masterson, we'll also learn that Trinidad was for 4 decades known as the sex change capital of the world. Here, in this unlikeliest of places, from the 1960s until 2003, Dr. Stanley Biber performed up to 4 operations a day on patients from all over the planet. Right about now, I could use a quadriceps change operation, not necessarily permanent, but a fresh change of muscle groups on temporary loan from, say, Tour de France champion Sir Bradley Wiggins. *Change is good, Bradley! Let's swap for just the next 4 days, okay? You can have a preview of what it's like to be 72, and I can enjoy a level of power I've never had and never will.* But, thank you, Trinidad. Change is good, and I am changing every mile, from fresh to fatigued, from slow to fast, from brimming optimism to dwindling hope and back again; all common denominators among the RAAM's immutable certainties.

Kayla Washburn

"Don was doing race simulation training days for the RAAM, and since he lived way up a dirt road, he asked Barney and me if he could use our house as his base for the day. He'd do twenty-minute rides spaced with twenty-

minute rests, for eight hours! He set up all his gear in the garage, food and drink mixes, both bikes, and a couple of dry sets of clothes, not necessarily clean clothes. We always pick on Don for using his bike kits as rags for cleaning his bike. It's normal to see fingerprints of grease on his bib shorts and a few smears of the blueberry Table Talk Pie he'd just replenished himself with on his jersey. So he set out on the road for an eight-hour session of what he expected the RAAM to be like every day. I drove past him on my way to work (and again on my way home). The forecast called for rain on and off all day. I honked and got a wave accompanied by a big smile. I could only imagine how painfully boring his day was going to be, but was inspired by his ambition and dedication to his teammates and their Race Across America.

Being a cyclist is kind of a funny thing. You think you want to start riding a bike, so you go out and get one. Friends who have no understanding of (and probably no interest in) the cycling scene think you're some kind of animal, but you soon realize, once you've been on a group ride, that you might as well be a boat anchor. This was my personal experience. I wanted to be able to ride with the pack. The 'B' ride was fine. The drop-you-like-a-hot-'tater, 'A' ride is full of socially awkward, Rocky-mentality, fast-as-all-get-out riders. It took me several years to get to the point where I could hang with most of my friends. I wasn't dedicated enough to get much faster and 'hanging' was a relative term. I'd gotten good at drafting, but the second the climbs began, 'boat anchor' was off the back! Don is (cough) forty (cough) three (cough, cough) years older than me, but he'll kick my ass up any hill, anywhere, any day. We always say, 'We hope we're in as good shape as Don when we're his age,' but at just a couple of years younger, we're not there even now!

I clearly remember United4Health's first day of the race. I was already checking the RAAM website every couple of hours to see what U4H's average speed was. I knew they had to beat an average of 16.03 mph, and it was common knowledge that they were hoping to come in over 18mph. I had just gotten off the phone with Barney early Sunday morning, and he told me the boys were flying and averaging over 20 mph. I was so proud of the old geezers! Don is my friend, but I had only been filled in on the characters of the three other men on the team. They were all heroes in my eyes. So, as I set out for a ride that same Sunday, a beautiful June morning in the Green Mountains of Vermont, I said to myself, 'I'm gonna try to ride as fast as I can and see if I can get my average close to theirs'. I rode for 3 hours, and 16.6 mph was my best effort. I couldn't stop thinking about all their hard work and dedication, the reasons why each of them were doing it, the support they all had/have from their loved ones. Were they trying to prove something? I couldn't imagine it was just for the fun of it, but then, what is the definition of fun?

I talked to Barney about once a day. I knew it was starting to become more inconvenient for him to call home as the days went on. Between trying to navigate, getting the racers ready for their transition, and being quiet in the RV so as not to wake the sleeping beauties, there never was a good time to catch up. As the days went on, it was more about survival for the crew. Sleepless nights, exhaustion, unforeseen problems, and not to mention catering to some self-centered, high maintenance racers. Little did I know it would take weeks for the crew to recover from the exhaustion.

I wanted to be at the finish line in Annapolis when United4Health came in. I booked my flight a few weeks in advance in order to arrive on Friday, determined not to miss the action. The only problem was, when would they finish? If they were as fast as their 18mph goal, they'd get in around 3 on Saturday afternoon, in time to clean up for Elena's celebration dinner. But from the start, their average speed was more in the 19+ mph range, so I started to get worried I wouldn't be there in time. Instead of having a day-plus to wander around Annapolis and check things out, I had only a few hours on Friday and then got up at 3 on Saturday morning to cheer them across the finish line at 4:40."

I spot a sign as we cross a bridge over the Purgatoire River. I can't see how deep or wide the water is in the darkness below, but I wish I hadn't seen the sign. Why was the river named Purgatoire? Purgatory is a place or state of temporary pain, torment or distress. Will crossing this river become a correlative for our RAAM ordeal? I tell myself to stop the two-bit superstitions, ignore this trashy ideation, get back to work and *pedal*. But between the darkness of the night, the 56 hours of accumulated fatigue and passing by the site of Breedlove's tragedy, I'm skittering along the edge of a purgatory of my own making.

A couple of hours before dawn in eastern Colorado, I see a flash low in the sky, far ahead. It appears, vanishes and then reappears. Due to the darkness, I have no idea of the topography around us, so I assume what I see are headlights on a twisty mountain road above us. Assumptions of any sort at 3 in the morning, after 1,100 miles of the RAAM, are suspect at best, but the assumptions are mine and cannot be denied. When I trade places with Dur and get back into the van, I ask Taylor and Chris if they saw the lights. They did not. I also ask if we are heading up into higher elevations and am relieved, albeit somewhat perplexed, when Taylor assures me we're not, so I retire my headlights-on-a-twisty-mountain-road assumption and enjoy one of chef Manny's avocado and cheese wraps from the cooler. Considering the dark, the hour and the work we've done since our shift began, it's refreshing to know that the mountains are finally behind us and we are about to begin the 600-mile slide into the flat-plate monotony of the Great Plains. The next real mountains we'll see will be in West Virginia, 1,500 miles away.

We leapfrog by Dur and speed another 15 minutes down the road where we'll make the tradeoff. As Dur comes into sight and I'm about to get on my bike, I turn and see the lights again, unmistakable now. Chris and Taylor see them, too. We watch in silence as a row of them, 3 or 4 wide, move across our view. "What's up with that?" Taylor says.

"Twilight Zone," Chris says. *"Creepy."*

The moment Dur pulls in beside me I accelerate away from the van in pursuit of this luminous phantom. I was cautious back on the stretch passing Bob Breedlove's tragedy, but now, an early-morning, subversive logic suggests that my curiosity entitles me to recklessness despite my pledge to play it safe. At least the roads are smooth and level, I'm making good time, and the danger quotient is low, so I pedal on auto pilot and keep one eye on the sky in front of me. In the next mile or two, I am almost directly under the lights. They move slowly in what appears to be about a half-mile in one direction and then swerve sharply and reverse course. If I were to assume the grade was flat between us, they would be about 100 ft. off the ground. Despite myself, I can't help but wonder: *Am I seeing a fucking UFO?*

The hype surrounding the 1950s' spaceship crash in Roswell, NM, never seemed remotely authentic to me. I need to see theories proven three times in a white room before my instinctive skepticism relents. I was over Santa Claus at 3; the Easter Bunny never had a chance. Those

Abducted-by-Aliens headlines in supermarket checkout tabloids are stupid fun to read, but I also see them as a tragic reminder that some tabloid readers believe every word -- *and vote.* Yes, we've all seen lights in the night sky we couldn't explain, but the Alien Spaceship default position is way too reductive for me. Until now. *Now,* I am convinced I'm witnessing a genuine UFO. Yes, I am dog-tired and it is an un-Godly hour of the night and I have no idea where in hell I am, but I absolutely see two pairs of bright lights moving at what appears to be 40-50 mph back and forth above me, and it is a beautiful, inexplicable sight. I can even hear what sounds like a motor propelling this marvel. *Why shouldn't UFO's have motors?* I wish I had my camera. How amazing that this Race Across America would include a UFO sighting! The next pass of my UFO brings it low over my head. I glance back at the follow van, take one hand off the handlebars and point urgently upward, sharing the miracle, gathering witnesses. When I reach the racer van and cross wheels with Dur, I yell, "Did you see that?" As usual, he's so focused on the race (which is, after all, what we came here to do) that he rides off without answering.

Chris and Taylor no longer seem impressed. "Crop duster," Chris says. "I'd love to fly one of those birds." He's an enthusiastic recreational pilot. "They fly before dawn to take advantage of the dew. Makes the pesticides stick better."

"To your lungs," Taylor says. "Don't breathe."

I exhale deeply, and chalk up another one to Colorado RAAMbrain.

It's too dark to see much except the road ahead, and its features are monotonously limited. Tonight, it seems that the reduction of visual stimulation enhances other senses, especially sound and smell. An hour or so after my naive UFO sighting, the familiar noise of my bike invades my senses as never before. When I listen carefully, I can distinguish between the whisper-hiss of tires on smooth pavement and the whisper-rasp of tires on slightly less smooth surfaces. The whirring chain's volume and pitch vary according to speed. The rush of air around my body and helmet depends upon my position. Tucked in and positioned down low, it's *piano*, soft and predictable. Sitting up tall and using my frontal area as a secondary brake at a stop sign, it becomes *forte*, loud and messy. If a tail wind blows at the same rate as the forward-travel speed, the only sound intruding into the silence of still air is mechanical. When the wind is head-on, the raucous rush of air overwhelms all mechanical sounds. And on the few occasions when I get to coast downhill, the ratcheting pawls in the free-wheeling rear hub make a serial clicking that sounds like metallic cicadas. Tuning into this little symphony of night music helps relieve the sameness of 95 miles between Trinidad and Pritchett, for besides pedaling hard, there's not much else in the way of entertainment.

For the first 70 miles of this high, dry country, we're up and down dozens of short hills, nothing brutal, but bunched together with few flat miles between them. The dark-of-night smells in these hills change with altitude. At the bottom of the dips, the air is noticeably cooler and holds hints of damp earth. Going over the peaks, the air is more active and dry and still scented with smoke from the forest fires far to the north. Whether it's better at night to actively engage in these sensory observations or turn everything off and dwell in the zone of meditative mindlessness may not even be a choice. This is my second all-night ride and it's increasingly difficult to concentrate on any one subject or focus on cadence and speed as much as I assumed I could.

I'm beginning to wonder if the RAAM's mental challenges are in some ways becoming equal to its physical, but then I remind myself that these two hours before daylight are the always the toughest.

Traveling eastward into the rising sun reminds me we are traveling against a two centuries'-old tide of New-World, westward migration. If we could only know the endless waves of seekers flowing from east to west, how would our hardships and motives compare with theirs? Beginning with the French trappers and traders, and on to the Lewis and Clark expedition of 1805, to the thousands of German/Scandinavian immigrants, to the homesteaders, outlaws, sodbusters, cattle barons, sheep ranchers, gold rushers, buffalo hunters, card sharks, con men, Indian fighters, Mormons, dreamers, dust bowl refugees and wanna-be Hollywood starlets -- how do we compare? Many suffered much more than we will, some suffered less. Our venture is idiosyncratic, ego-driven and historically inconsequential. We have little to lose, and we enjoy multiple safeguards against danger. For personal reasons, we've driven ourselves hard to achieve an ephemeral goal, a sense of satisfaction, a number in a record book and bragging rights in life's lavish locker rooms. The extreme physical difficulties we put ourselves through are life-affirming, inspirational, healthy and harmless to others. For me, these are all defensible, while at the same time, indefensible as *necessities*. Our pioneers' goals were driven by critical economic, religious and political forces that placed the fortunes and lives of entire communities at risk. They journeyed westward with hopes of beginning a better future. We travel eastward with hopes of adding the thrill of a lifetime to our remarkably fortunate lives. I imagine the only motive we have in common is the promise we've all made to follow our dreams.

As the week progresses, I realize I'm spending about

6 hours out of every 24 with the racer van crew, Chris Champion, Nate Keck and Taylor Keaton, more awake time with them than with anyone else, including Dur. I like being in the van with them. Two are on duty at all times; each works a 16-hour shift, swapping driving and navigation duties every 8 hours. The third crew member's shift is offset so that the combination is always changing -- e.g. Nate + Taylor x 8 hrs. followed by Taylor + Chris x 8 hrs. followed by Chris +Nate x 8 hrs. Repeat this sequence 19 times from Oceanside to Annapolis and you get the idea: it's *exhausting*. They're tasked with night and day driving, navigating every turn correctly, calling in to each of the 54 time stations placed at irregular intervals along the route, finding legal pull-offs every 20-25 minutes, unloading the outgoing racer's bike, safely guiding the incoming rider to the tradeoff point, seeing the outgoing racer safely en route, securing the incoming racer's bike to the rack on the back of the van, getting the incoming rider safely into the van, leapfrogging the outgoing racer and follow van -- and proceeding to the next rider swap, 6 -7 miles down the road. Add to these duties the logistics of keeping themselves fed and rested, the van cleaned and fueled, dealing with malfunctioning communication systems, intermittent cell reception, unforeseen course changes and the occasional grumpy racer bitching about something that can't be helped, and you come up with three candidates for canonization. It also becomes clear they've been instructed not to discuss racers with racers even though, or perhaps, especially because, no one knows more about us than they do and the information shared could be divisive or demoralizing. Yes, they are discreet. If I ask how a teammate is doing, I get a positive/neutral response, transparently opaque, diplomatically inexact, exactly what it should be.

The racer van drivers are not the only Saints in this challenging Church of Perpetual Pedaling. Driving, fueling and cleaning the stinky, lumbering RVs is also a staggering chore. Barney and Michael of the racer RV have nicknamed it "the hearse," for reasons I don't want to examine too closely. A recurring inquiry under their jurisdiction is the question of who crapped in the racer RV's ostensibly out-of-order toilet. I continue to plead innocent and can neither confirm nor deny allegations that it was one or several or none of my esteemed teammates. I can, however, willingly attest to the presence of unseemly aromas and many, many flies in our humble castle on wheels, but I'm usually too fatigued to mind.

Lewis and Howard in the crew RV also deserve Bike Heaven Beatification for their remarkable energy, patience and ability to keep their warp-speed driving under the constabulary's radar, but both the RV's sagas pale compared to the Tales From The Follow Van.

Ken Gunnells

"Before the race begins in Oceanside CA, I pick up a pebble from the beach, take a picture of it and put it in my pocket.

Follow van life goes like this: Crawling along behind the racers, the hazard blinkers are always ticking. It drives you crazy. Near the end, I am singing songs to the beat. Ma-ry-had-a-lit-tle-lamb. . . Over the days of the race, all the social niceties get washed away and you really get to know the person you are working with. With our 16-hr driving schedule, there is not much time to get to know other crew members beyond their names and a little personal information.

On the RAAM 4 years ago, I figured out how to program off-the-shelf GPSs to follow the exact RAAM route. Now, these GPSs are our constant companions. We name the one in the follow van Ruby, (don't take your love to town) and the one in racer van, Wanda The Crazy Bitch, because she keeps crashing. We navigate by double-checking the route book with the GPS. Sometimes the GPS clarifies a route book instruction, sometimes the route book clarifies what the GPS is showing. I also have the route on my iPhone in Google Earth as a backup, which saves us at a midnight intersection in Ohio, when the book and GPS both have us confused around new road construction.

Before sunset each evening, we have to make sure we have enough fuel to get us through the night. Running out of gas is not an option. My typical shift begins before sunset and ends mid-morning. We have to stay close to the racer at night, so we can't take the time to stop and pee. We drink less and learn to hold it. By the end of the race I am significantly dehydrated. The hours of 2, 3 and 4 a.m. are always the worst, the monotony of the blinkers going tick, tick, tick, tick, tick, and you can't see anything but the racer in your headlights. Michael Patterson has a pair of cycling shorts that have a little red tab sticking out right on the middle of his ass. At night, the red tab swings back and forth in our headlights, tick, tick, tick, 18-20 mph. . . mesmerizing.

As soon as I get off shift, I hop in a bunk in the crew's RV while it takes off to the next transition and I'm bounced down the road, in and out of maybe 4-5 hours of so-called sleep. As the next shift approaches I eat a little, hope to find a bathroom and food for next day and use disinfectant wipes on my face, underarms, crotch, and feet. No matter how hard I try, or how often I am reminded I need to stay awake, sometimes the body says no. A couple of times, I drive my shift and most of the next shift. I was once so exhausted I fell asleep in the navigator's seat. When John tried to rouse me, I couldn't be awakened. He later told me he feared I was dead. When I finally woke up, I couldn't remember who I was or where I was. It was a half hour before I could carry on a conversation, and over an hour before I could remember how to do my job.

Combine this constant fatigue with maintaining the recommended following distance at night (Dave Eldridge recommends that 'You should see a little pavement between the back tire of the bike and your hood.'), and you have a potentially dangerous situation. On the climbs and flats we can maintain our protective role staying directly behind the racer. On fast descents, we stay close behind but off to the left so that our headlights shine more in front of the racer and we have less risk of overrunning him. Occasionally, during fast descents on curvy roads, we use a powerful spot light to provide illumination farther around a curve.

The PA system on the follow van is a constant problem. At the beginning we expected to talk easily to the racers, and play them music. But due to feedback, distortion, and the deafness in some racers' ears, it never works as expected. Some racers tolerate it and seem to appreciate what we are trying to do, some gesture rudely and complain.

Dave Eldridge underestimated the need for van-to-van communication and thought that cell phones would suffice -- but I don't think they do. There is an almost constant need for short, quick communications. (How far away are you? Blink your lights, so I know it's you. We're going to get gas, etc.) Dave buys us some cheap walkie-talkies, but they only work when they are less than a mile apart.

In Kansas, he buys a set of CB radios, but their performance is not much better. In the end I find myself driving with the CB mic in one hand and the PA mic in the other, sometimes getting confused about which I should be talking into.

I think the race is lost when Dave Burnett has heat

stroke and dehydration in Parker, CA. There is a lot of painful climbing to be watched from my follow-van as the other racers take up the slack. I remember watching Don dutifully get on his bike and steadily climb some of the worst climbs I've ever seen. Spirits seem low, but Don, Dur and Michael keep going, and then Dave is back and raring to go at the start of the night shift from Tuba City."

Miles before we get to the team exchange in Pritchett, CO, I see 3 giant grain silos interrupting the flat horizon. The distance between us is so vast and undifferentiated that it's impossible to measure progress in less than 10-minute increments. The road, the barbed wire fences and the infinite sea of grasslands define the sum total of this landscape. As I pedal on, I might as well be crossing a gently rippling ocean, lured in by a trio of lighthouses. It's here that for the first time I connect the adjective "plain" with the noun. These Plains are some of the plainest places I've ever seen, a prelude to the ultimate Plain-ness of Kansas.

The 170-mile shift ends for Dur and me at team exchange #8 in Pritchett, CO, at 7 in the morning. We're tired, but our average speed from the last time station in Trinidad is almost 19 mph, so, considering the conditions, we're happy enough as Michael takes off into the cool morning air followed by Dave in the racer van.

Jan Smolowitz

"I distinctly remember the drastic changes in the landscape, from the green fields and flowers in Colorado to the stale stench of manure in Kansas. According to the RAAM route book, 'Rolling ranch lands of eastern Colorado metamorphose into unexpectedly flat farm land.' They didn't mention that right off the sides of the road, pens were filled with thousands of cattle with not a blade of

grass in sight. I focused on finding and checking off every mile marker to avoid thinking about my surroundings. The markers kept referring to specific grain elevators, clearly the tall, round structures at the side of the road. However, I couldn't find a name on a single one and wasn't sure how I would know where to turn based on these route book instructions. Here's an example of some of the most important set of (baffling) instructions: **'Very gradual descending continues. Don't miss the turn at mile 11.7: Don't enter Ensign on US 56. When Ensign grain elevators come into view you are on a very straight section of US56 E. The next turn is onto an inconspicuous 2-lane road just as US 56 starts to bend to the left. 11.7: Turn right Ford Ensign Road (marked only by a standard yellow cross road caution sign) before US 56 curves left toward town of Ensign. If you immediately pass a school on your left you made the correct turn, but if the school is on your right you missed the turn and getting back isn't easy.'** *I was in the crew RV, trying to make sense of the route book. The driver and I disagreed on the road best taken, so we just stopped the RV on the road where the routes diverged.(Robert Frost -- hello?) The driver asked me to call the racer RV and request their opinion. The racer RV navigator replied, 'We've been hoping you knew what you were doing, and are following you.' Luckily, we made the correct decision and proceeded."*

While Dur and I sleep, Michael and Dave are murdering the miles coming into Kansas. They've lucked out with a tail wind that will soon turn hostile and come at us sideways from the south, but for now, with a wind assist and a constant downhill drop of 2,500 ft., they open up a can of Whup-Ass and ride the wheels off their bikes at 24-25 mph!

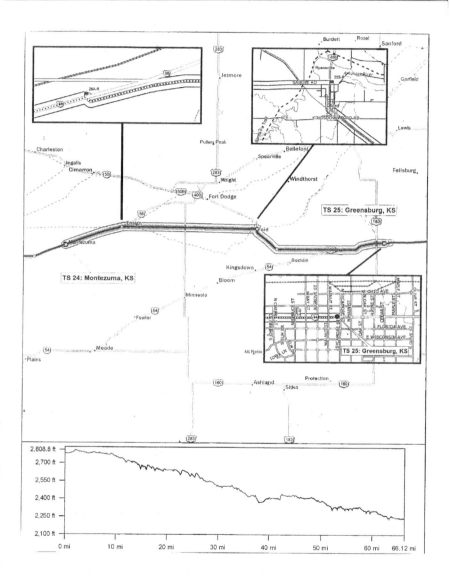

Jan Smolowitz

"Near the end of our pull into Ford, KS, the last perplexing set of instructions was: **'Mile 11.8 –School on left. Mile 38.6 turn right:1SS: US 400E (unmarked)'** *The instructions seemed pretty clear. We would travel straight and turn right on an unmarked road in 20 miles. How or why it was a U.S. designated highway and left unmarked may simply be that in such a sparsely populated place, everybody knows where they're going, so why put up a sign? There were no comments about surrounding landmarks. I assumed we would be traveling a long way down a lonely road and there would be an intersection in 20 miles. Wrong. Unmarked roads constantly intersected this narrow two-lane we were on. The land was flat fields on either side of the road for as far as I could see. I was doubly concerned because there was a slight variance in our odometer and the mile markers. What if we missed the unmarked turn? How would we know? I must have voiced my concerns to the driver a few times too many. A resting crew member overheard the conversation and dropped down from the overhead platform. He pulled out the global GPS on his phone and showed me satellite photos of our RV traveling through waves of grass being blown by gusting cross winds. This was at about the same time that I heard the riders were starting to suffer the wind, and I reverted to prayer.*

We somehow found the unmarked road, turned down it and soon were parked between a gas station and the Blue Hereford Restaurant, the only visible businesses in town. It was so windy, I had to walk sideways to get to the restaurant. It would be a while before the riders came in, but I couldn't imagine how they could maintain their pace in this wind."

Karen Scheerer

"I'm a retired Nursing Home Administrator and I've been a crewmember in 3 Races Across America. Two of the three races resulted in record-setting finishes. In 2011, I crewed for a group of 10, Type 1 diabetic (Team Type 1) runners who Ran Across America non-stop in 15 days from Oceanside, California to New York City, finishing on World Diabetes Day. I've functioned in a variety of roles during each race: Mom, Photographer, Navigator, Pre-Race Organization, Post-Race Finish Clean-Up, Cook, Grocery Getter, Laundry lady and general helper to whoever needs it. At home, I'm a Mom to three kids, a Mimi to 4 grand kiddies, a wife and a daughter.

Success in the RAAM isn't possible without strong racers and a committed crew. Dave Eldridge takes charge of finding those people who can work hard with minimal sleep, keep their heads on straight, live on food from gas station vending machines, bathe once or twice a week and live in the same clothes for days at a time. There are a lot of people who don't make the cut. Those who do are fine people, and the Race Across America starts some amazing, lifelong friendships. For me, the race starts when I get a call from crew chief Dave Eldridge, about 12 months before the event begins. Then the daily work begins, identifying ideal locations for transition exchanges, going to Google maps, plugging in the route and zooming in on roads all across the country, searching for open spaces large enough to park RVs and allow enough space to set up 'camp' until the racers arrive. Local Laundromats, healthcare facilities, pharmacies, eateries, restrooms, and grocery stores need to be identified. I put all this information into a spreadsheet and turn it over to Dave, who then calculates racer arrival times at each exchange location. Dave and I also work on a procedure book that communicates to all crew and racers what they have gotten themselves into. If this hasn't scared anyone off, we wait, answer questions, and continue to fine-tune details until we arrive in California two days before the race begins.

For 6 days, I sleep in the front passenger seat of the support van with my legs out the window, covered by a sleeping bag. Dave does most of the driving while I navigate and take racer photos, sometimes just hanging out the window for action shots and a breath of fresh air. A big moment for me is watching Dave Burnett climb over the Continental Divide at 10,856 feet elevation in Colorado. His display of strength and energy is one of the most emotional moments for me of the entire race. I become attached to this group of strangers way before they ever know who I am. At the finish line, as exciting as it is, it is also somewhat sad. Knowing that this group has worked so hard under the most difficult of circumstances for the last six days makes their sudden departure difficult for me. I have such fond memories of these inspirational, 2012 RAAM racers and crew; they will always have a place in my heart."

"... For age is opportunity no less
Than youth itself, though in another dress,
And as the evening twilight fades away
The sky is filled with stars, invisible by day."

Henry Wadsworth Longfellow

DAY FOUR
Ford, KS to Mokane, MO
487 miles

My first view of Kansas unfolds through the fly-specked windows of the RV, late in the day on June 19th. It's the beginning of the 4th day since we set out from the balmy, palm-lined beach beside the Pacific Ocean. We've left California, Arizona, Utah and Colorado behind us and are currently 175 miles south of the geographic center of the lower 48 states. In another 100 miles, we'll be half-way between Oceanside and Annapolis.

The crew has set up camp in a vacant parking lot in downtown Ford, pop. 216, where today's temperature reaches an unapologetic 100 F. Ford lies about 15 miles SE of Dodge City, home to Wyatt Earp and Doc Holliday. In the late 1870s, millions of Texas Longhorn cattle were shipped from Dodge City to eastern markets on the Santa Fe Railroad. And even though we never enter Dodge City's city limits, the clichéd gunslinger's rebuke to "Get out of Dodge" becomes an apt mantra over the next 260 miles. Long before we've crossed it, Kansas will be our least favorite cycling state.

The Kansas state motto is *Ad Astera per Aspera*, "To the Stars through Difficulties." Originally part of the Louisiana Purchase of 1803, Kansas became the 34th State in 1861, and the motto proved to be an apt summation of this border state's many frontier struggles. Abolitionist John Brown's battles with pro-slavery factions are believed to have triggered a series of events that led to the Civil War. On our long and arduous ride across the Sunflower State, we see plenty of stars and encounter our share of difficulties. Our motto would more suitably be, *Ad **Annapolis** per Aspera*.

We're parked along Rte 400, next to the Blue Hereford restaurant. With Michael and Dave's estimated arrival more than an hour away, Barney, Michael Scholl and I head over for a meal and the use of the bathroom. Proper bathrooms are a treasured commodity on the RAAM. The lack of time to find legal RV disposal facilities means that our RVs' toilets are useless. So, while there's always a tree or a boulder to stand behind, sitting down requires the opportunistic use of gas stations, convenience stores and restaurant rest rooms. Although no one conducts a survey, it seems that somehow or other, (most of) our 19 person armada manages to find public bathrooms all the way across America.

Ford's restaurant is almost as big as the town itself, and nearly as empty. Three other customers sit among the dozens of tables despite the approaching dinner hour. We pick a booth with a view out the window and watch a tree being twisted sideways by the wind. There are probably other trees bent crooked in the wind as well, but none that we can see between us and the distant horizon. I'd heard the expression *"You can see all the way across Kansas -- but not from here,"* and now I get it. Sunflowers, fence posts, windmills, grain silos and oil rigs are the predominant vertical shapes.

Over by the kitchen, a pair of waitresses huddle in conversation. A few minutes pass before they notice us, so we talk about the danger of lateral wind loads against deep-profile wheels and continue staring out the window, mesmerized by the buffeted tree and collectively wondering, *Does it ever stop?* The RV crew has been following weather reports all day and the forecasts are ominous: winds out of the south gusting up to 40 mph with no let-up in sight. If the current trajectory continues, we will lose significant speed and expend a lot of extra energy just fighting to stay upright. If the wind shifts slightly and comes towards us from a more easterly direction, we're going to be hurting badly. Riding into 40 mph gusts could bring our speed down to 5 mph and turn a 14-hour ride into a full day's sufferfest. The hopeful scenario is for these gusts to shift to a tail wind and fly us down the road, but no one dares to have much faith in that scenario. Today is the first time I've overheard chief Eldridge and the crew so outspoken about a threat to our success, but this wind across Kansas is blowing so hard it's impossible to ignore.

I've never put much faith in weather predictions. For me, a 70% chance of rain is just as likely to mean a 30% chance of sunshine. In New England, we say, *"If you don't like the weather, just wait a minute."* I like that approach and hope it will apply here in Kansas. And anyway, what choice do we have but to get on the bikes and ride? My cavalier attitude may be due to a lack of imagination, fatigue or laziness, but since the weather forecast is beyond my control, I focus on something that is: a tray of pies across the room. The blueberry looks ravishing. We've been burning 6 or 7,000 calories a day, and today is the first and last time we'll luck into a sit-down restaurant. Crew chef Manny does a great job feeding us on the road, but deep dish blueberry pie is beyond the scope of his makeshift kitchen. When the waitress takes our orders, I decide to wash down the pie with black coffee, a double cheeseburger, gravy biscuits, steak fries and coleslaw.

We're woefully watching the wind-whipped tree across the highway when 2 oil-field workers walk in and sit down in the booth next to us. Their friendly conversation with the waitress suggests they are regular customers; it's easy to imagine they all went to high school together, that everybody in a small town like Ford knows everybody else. I feel kind of delicate next to these tall, beefy guys who are big enough to be 2 of me and young enough to be my grandsons. I also notice how relieved I am to be dressed in civvies. These guys are sporting Carhartt overalls, size XXL, and Caterpillar steel-toed boots. When they encounter cyclists on the road, dressed in shiny, skin-tight, bright-colored kits, with shaved legs and dainty cycling shoes, I can understand how they might think of them as effeminate. But if they had an opportunity to ride a mile -- or 3,000 -- in those dainty shoes, how would that change their thinking? Many of us have had our masculinity mocked by macho men driving by in jacked-up pickup trucks. If only we could answer with, *"You could be right, Bubba, but just for fun, let's trade. I'll sit in your truck and drive up the mountain and you pedal my bike, okay?"* Our cycling garb would be just as disastrous in oil-field work as Carhartts would be on a bike, but I want to think that what we have in common with these oil-field workers is a hard day's labor. This race across America is stupid-hard work that requires a delirious degree of stamina and discipline, and except for its voluntary nature -- admittedly, no small distinction -- it's not a whole lot different from every day, "real" hard work, which is what I assume these guys got up and did this morning out of pure necessity.

I've scraped the last trace of pie from my plate and I'm still hungry, but Barney reminds me that Michael and Dave are due in 45 minutes, and I need to digest my impulsive homage to fats and carbs. The food we've been served here at the Blue Hereford is delicious in the same way that a burnt hot dog is delicious if you're ten years-old on an overnight camping trip and you haven't eaten since you started up the mountain 6 hours ago with your much-too-heavy backpack. We over-tip the waitress in appreciation for this unique opportunity to sit down to a big meal, and as we pass the booth next to ours, I ask the oil-field guys what they think about the wind. They look up at me quizzically, probably wondering who these strangers are, what they're doing here in Ford and where they're going, but they are too polite to inquire. I re-phrase the question and ask if they think the wind will keep blowing all day or die down at night. Their friendly but offhand answer makes it apparent that the wind hereabouts is so commonplace that it barely deserves notice. When we walk outside and I feel the gusts tugging at my clothes, I take a long look at this notorious, pancake-flat state known for its straight roads, heat, humidity, thunderstorms and cyclones, and I'm tempted to climb back in the RV and sleep all the way to Missouri.

Michael and Dave pull into Ford exhausted but victorious. They've ridden 176 miles in less than 9 hours and posted our team's fastest splits. In the 95 miles from the team exchange in Pritchett, CO, they took advantage of a steady, 1,800-ft. drop in elevation all the way to Ulysses, KS, and averaged almost 25 mph. Coming through Montezuma, KS, the gusts began slowing them down, but they brought our total trip average up from 18.95 mph to19.25 mph. This is spectacular news. Riding 25 mph over a distance of 95 miles entitles cyclists of any age to bragging rights. Riding it at the age of 70 entitles these old boys to triple cheeseburgers. With bacon.

Howard Conway

"Manny Casillas was the nutritionist/cook for the racers. He was trying his best to cook up good food for them, but that was not easy. One racer in particular was fussy about food prep, not liking this, not liking that, not very good at getting along generally, and that grated on the crew. I think some of the crew were jealous that the racers got hot meals cooked for them while we ate crap -- peanut butter jelly

sandwiches, junk food, McDonald's, etc. I guess that was another thing that added to the tension, but I have to give kudos to Manny as he saved some lives late one night. It was the third night out and I had been working hard trying to make the racer exchanges go better as we were terrible with them early on. I also tried to stay up and soak up all the western scenery, and it caught up with me on my late night driving shift. It was about 4 a.m., pitch dark on some lonely road and I was so sleepy. Manny was navigating and I just could not stay awake. I drifted the RV into the other lane, dead asleep. Manny yelled and shook me, scared the crap out of me -- and him. Everyone else was so tired they slept on through it. I grabbed my Mountain Dew and Sugar Babies and made sure I stayed awake the rest of the trip."

There's a whippy wind coming out of the south when Dur and I leave Ford a few hours before sunset. We discuss with Nate and Chris whether it's better to use the faster, but less stable TT (time trial) bikes, or play it safer on our climbing/road bikes. We agree to experiment, and I start out on my Parlee TT. Wind is tough enough to deal with when it blows at a steady rate, but it won't do that today. Just when I find the optimum angle of lean into it, the velocity increases or decreases and I'm required to adjust the angle of lateral resistance. With no wind interference, the gyroscopic benefit of the rotating wheel mass keeps a bicycle going straight. The faster it goes, the straighter it goes, and the more resistant it is to turning. The problem with speed today is that when the wind rips the bike off its straight-line course, control is a serious challenge. These incessant, irregular, wind-induced corrections make it impossible to maintain a steady rhythm and require extra effort just to keep the wheels on the road.

Just east of Ford, Dur is riding and I'm in the van when we

pass through Mullinville, pop. 255. As we approach the little clutch of buildings, I see a tall, fence-like row of colorful folk sculpture bordering the north side of the highway, welded metal windmills, whirligigs and cartoonish politicians. Nate slows down so we can appreciate the hundreds of pieces. The artist, M.T. Ligget, is a retired farmer with outsized political views. It would take an hour to look at everything, but I catch glimpses of sculpture with hand-painted titles such as, *"Sen. Joe Biden, Sycophantic Plagiarist"*, and, *"Evolution Is Wrong"*, and, *"Hillary Clinton, Jack-booted Eva Braun"*. There's a black, oven-shaped sculpture topped off with swastikas and the words, *"Davidians"* and *"Waco"* and a cartooned, decapitated Janet Reno and, *"Never Again"*. These politicized images are offset with sculptures of grinning dogs, animated pumpkins and boot-shod chickens. I have a pang of regret that we can't stop and see Ligget's entire *oeuvre,* but we're moving down the highway, and within a few minutes I'm back in the saddle and RAAMing across Kansas at full throttle.

Leaving the sculpture of Mullinville, we follow the 2-lane Highway 54 most of the way across Kansas to the Missouri line. It runs parallel to, and about 90 miles south of I-70, and crosses I-35 in Wichita. Luckily for us, traffic on 54 is low-volume, but it is frequented by tractor trailer trucks going 70 mph. I quickly learn to distinguish the distant sound of these trucks, the increasing pitch of their road noise as they approach and the falling-off, Doppler effect when they whoosh by. When the first few overtake me from behind, I'm once again grateful to be protected by the follow van. The truck's passing speed, relative to mine at 18-20 mph, amounts to a 50+ mph advantage, but since we're travelling in the same direction, the air impact is relatively manageable and I even feel a momentary forward boost created by the volume of air sucked along behind the trailer. For that brief, windy moment, I'm effectively drafting off the side of an 18-wheeled peloton. But it's a different dynamic when a tractor trailer passes me head on. A big Kenworth cab hauling a 13ft.-high, 53 ft.-long box trailer (the combination of which can weigh up to 80,000 lbs.) displaces a huge volume of air in its path. The truck's 70 mph speed added to mine would mean the equivalent of 85-90 mph in a head-on crash. As it roars by, I first feel as if I've been slammed by a huge fist of angry air, and then yanked back toward it as turbulence implodes into the vacuum wake created behind the trailer. I quickly learn to dread these oncoming monster trucks and hug the side of the road when I see one coming.

While the 5-10-minute lulls between the big trucks are welcome a relief, the battle against the side wind never ends. It's ironic that the RAAM's route through Kansas is the straightest west-to-east line of any section we will travel. In Arizona and Colorado, we rode hundreds of miles pointed north, northeasterly, and if the wind had been coming at 40 mph from the south as it is today, we would have enjoyed effortless speeds of over 30 mph. Today, I find myself looking far down the road hoping to see a left-hand turn, a swing to the north for only a mile or two, anything to get this wind behind me and make it useful.

At the end of my first pull, Dur takes off on his P3 Cervelo TT bike and I get in the van and talk to Chris and Taylor about the scary handling characteristics of the Parlee. Because it's potentially faster, I agree to try it a few more turns. The Parlee could get me out of Dodge in a hurry if the wind would only stop. On flat, smooth roads, I love the ease of speed and sense of purpose in the TT design. A TT bike is first and foremost designed to go very fast on moderately straight, moderately level, smooth surfaces with little or no crosswinds. Its shape is driven by aerodynamics and rider bio-mechanics; speed matters most, comfort least.

For starters, time trial frames are wind-cheatingly slim from the front, but wide from the side, hence vulnerable to the impact of lateral winds. Resistance to the still air in front of a rider requires 80-90% of the energy needed to move the bicycle ahead: this resistance rises *exponentially* as velocity increases, so the less frontal area presented by the rider and bike, the faster you go. The TT rider's position is moved forward so that the rider's back is, ideally, parallel to the top tube, elbows supported in aero bar cups -- again, less frontal area. The forearms form a "V" and the finger tips approximate the point of a wedge. Wearing a skin suit and a tear-drop shaped helmet significantly decreases "drag" through the air, all of which means the rider could go 2-3 mph faster than on any other type of bike under the same conditions. On steep hills and twisty, bumpy, roads, however, the TT bike's greater weight, frame geometry and riding position are an extreme liability. Other disadvantages in these conditions include twitchy steering and the notoriously awkward, anatomically insulting TT saddles, known to make strong riders walk funny when they dismount. Cross winds on flat, straight roads such as these in Kansas present yet another problem with the TT bike when equipped with deep-profile wheels: they act like sails. For straight-ahead, ideal-condition aerodynamics, racers benefit significantly from wheels such as the ZIPP 404s or 808s, or even the solid-disc rear wheel, all of which are stocked in our combined team TT arsenal in the back of the racer van. (See bike specs at the back of the book). The only problem is the wind. The surface areas of these exotic wheels can double or triple the bike's wind-catching profile and blow a rider off the road. And they can *sing*.

Dur Higgins

"My TT bike had a new rear wheel and tire, a Zipp 808 Firecrest with a Continental Sprinter tubular tire. I brought it to use in lieu of the rear disc wheel I ordinarily use for time trial competitions. My front wheel is an older Zipp 808 with a Continental Competition 19mm tire rated for up to 180 psig. I was surprised at the loudness of the wheels and tires at high speed in Kansas. They sing! I suppose that the noise may not be any louder than I had heard in time trials, but I think the Firecrest wheel is louder. And the sound increases with speed. The noise was so loud and high-pitched it would probably require earplugs in an industrial setting. My tires were inflated to 160 psig which would contribute to the high pitch and rough ride. And I think these tires are silicon rubber which I have observed to be louder."

Aside from the wind, there's another evil lurking. Starting in eastern Colorado, an increasing number of the roads we travel are segmented, built with expansion joints every 50-75 feet. About 10% percent of our RAAM route passes over such segmented roads, 300 guaranteed-to-be-nasty miles regardless of steep slopes or bad weather. These transverse belts are what create the micro-bumps that punctuate a passenger car's travel with a harmless little *ka-thunk, ka-thunk*. The problem is, we're not in a 4,000 lb passenger car with soft suspension and 30 psi tires. We're riding with no suspension on skinny tires and our vehicles weigh less than a cocker spaniel. Aboard the Parlee, I'm hunched over into the thinly-padded, weight-bearing elbow cups, and every 5 seconds or so the interminable *ka-thunks* send a jolt up through my shoulders and neck and into the occipital ridge at the back of my head. It's so painful it makes my teeth hurt. The only remedy is to lift my elbows out of the cups and straighten my arms, but that makes steering in the wind even more precarious, increases my profile to the wind and unnaturally strains my shoulders and back.

Dur Higgins

"The wind was mostly perpendicular to our route with a bit of a head-on component. But the problem was the way it would suddenly gust very hard, trying to blow the bike from the right hand shoulder of the road over into the on-coming traffic. During my first pulls, I was on the brake hoods much of the time which minimizes the TT bike advantage. I finally went to my road bike, as did Don, and we continued much of our shift on our road bikes. We were slower on road bikes but we just did not feel safe on the TTs during that stretch.

In Kansas, the tall grass bends over the road's edge and serves as a good visual pointer, so you can easily tell the wind's angle to the road. As our shift went on, the angle slowly changed from a slight headwind to an occasional tailwind, but the strong side gusts ruled the day. Added to the wind was the problem of transverse cracks, which extend all the way across the road. Due to thermal cycling of the asphalt caused by the sun, they become wide with a raised lip. Hitting these cracks on my TT bike was extremely jarring. With 160 psi air pressure in the 19mm front tire, mounted on a deep profile wheel, which does not flex much, the ride was brutal. That, plus with a short HB stem and my elbows down in the handlebar cups, my head took the shock of each crack and it felt like my brain was tearing loose from my skull. And the faster I hit the cracks the worse it felt. These repetitive cracks would occur for indeterminate stretches on roads all the way from Colorado to Ohio. You never knew when they would begin or end, but when they did end, a smooth, normal road felt so good. On the days when we used the TT bikes a lot, my neck would become very stiff and sore from being held up so hard for so long. When I would dismount the bike I could hardly stand the pain and I'm sure the Racer Van crew got tired of hearing my moans and groans as I gingerly crawled into the back seat holding my neck. The first time it happened, Nate was so concerned he got into the back seat and massaged my neck. After that I think he figured I was just going to have to tough it out, because, as he said, he did not hire on as a masseuse."

The interesting thing about those first few hours from the Blue Hereford Restaurant in Ford is that, aside from M.T. Ligget's folk sculpture, there's nothing much interesting left to see. Miles of flat pastureland on both sides of the road give no rest to the eye and no protection from the wind, no trees, no hedgerows, nothing but barbed wire fences and a few lonely cattle to lessen the unrelenting weight of wind. This land was once home to the Arapaho, Osage, Kiowa, and Comanche who hunted, trapped and fought for their lives on these endless plains. Looking at a map today, the hundreds of named Kansas counties and towns are predominantly Anglo-Saxon in origin. Only a few dozen Indian references -- Wichita, Pottawatomie, Pawnee Rock, Comanche, Cheyenne, Wabaunsee -- are among the scant remains of the state's native heritage. Stranger still is the nation-wide use of the name *Montezuma.* Within the 12 states the RAAM crosses, 8 of them, stretching from California eastward to Illinois, Indiana and Ohio, have towns, counties or natural resources named after the Aztec emperor *Moctezuma,* murdered by Cortes in 1520.

Howard Conway

"The wind in Kansas was awful. We parked the RV's in a V, pointed into the wind trying to block the current of air so we could sit outside the RV's while others slept. There was never enough room for the crew to sleep all at once. Somebody had to be outside the RV if they were awake so others could sleep. I had a fold up chair in a bag and the wind picked the canvas bag up and blew it way down into a corn field and I walked down to pick it up and the grit in the wind just made you feel like you were being sandblasted. I could not imagine what the racers were feeling on the course. We were parked in an old gas station next to the old pumps with an awning over the area and I swear I thought the awning was going to blow off. When I drove through KS, I had the wheel turned 30 degrees into the wind pointing the tires against the wind so we would stay on the road, it was a fight all the way driving those high profile rigs through the wind. I was glad to get out of Kansas. I have no idea why Dorothy, in the Wizard of Oz, wanted to go home to Kansas. There is nothing but wind, farms, cows and more wind. Talk about a miserable place in the winter in a snowstorm. All I ever saw in Kansas interesting was the wind farms. Those were awesome and we went fairly close to some and you could hear the blades swishing as they were turning, pretty awesome sound to hear and beautiful sight to see."

When the Spanish brought horses to the New World in the 1500s, it was the Comanche who seized the horseback advantage and became the exceptional horsemen among native peoples. Comanche County, on the Oklahoma border southeast of Ford, commemorates the tribe's presence in Kansas. Cunning tacticians in battle, they dominated the plains for decades with their new-found horseback riding skills. As I scan the horizon from my high-tech, carbon fiber bicycle, I wonder what they saw when they looked off into the distance, and how much of that I'm missing. I wonder how fast their war ponies could run, how far they could travel in a day, and I wonder how they chose their travel routes? In hilly topographies, the first and foremost pathways between places follow watercourses and cross rivers and mountain passes at the most auspicious locations. Here on the flat, plain plains, there are few of those features. Did the sun and stars provide their navigational clues? Or could they also count on the wind as a capricious, substitute compass?

Our average speed for the first 40 miles is a discouraging 15 mph. When night falls and the road surface improves, we ride the TT bikes again and do the best we can to trick the wind in our favor, but the effort is immense considering the measly return. And as if to remind us of the futility of hope, the segmented creases begin again and it's back to the road bikes. I find myself worrying that Michael and Dave, after their spectacular ride into Ford, will wonder if we're dogging it tonight, but I know Dur isn't, and if I am, it sure feels like some of the hardest work on the trip so far. Chris and Taylor in our racer van and John and Greg in the follow van must be discouraged to see us moving so slowly, but at least they know why, as their vans are being wind-buffeted, too.

Mason Poe of the Wounded Warriors Team 4 Mil

"I was unfamiliar with the RAAM (as well as cycling in general) until May 2011 when I was asked to crew for Team 4 Mil. I supported the team as a navigator/driver of the "Utility Vehicle" and was able to be part of Team 4 Mil's mission, outlook and goal in supporting our entire Military. I also learned they wanted to be first American team of wounded veterans to successfully complete the RAAM in 2012, and I wanted to be part of it.

In November of 2011, I purchased a used road bike from the 2011 RAAM crew chief, Marine Veteran Tony Serrano, who served in the US Marine many years prior to my enlistment. Tony and I immediately had a lot in common and were good friends as soon as he said he is a Marine, because there is no such thing as a former Marine. "Once a Marine, Always a Marine", and this is very true to all those that earned the right to don the US Marine Corps Emblem, 'Eagle, Globe and Anchor'.

I started in January, 2012 to ride the bike 6 days a week, but I didn't know the proper way to train so I just got on the bike and pedaled. In March, Jim Weinsten, the 2011 RAAM team Captain, took me under his wing and coached me on how long and how intense he wanted my daily rides to be, etc. I did what he suggested, and after just 5 months, I was physically ready and felt the best I had felt since the amputation of my right leg below the knee in 2004 and the subsequent 6 1/2 years of limb salvage completed in June of 2010. So, two years after my final amputation procedures, I was going to be on a team consisting of 8 veterans with only 12 working legs, and we were going to ride the longest endurance bike race in the world!

The question I had for myself was, how many blisters will my residual limb develop? Will I be able to keep my average speed up as fast as possible on the 5th, 6th or 7th day? I'm even asking myself if I am going to be able to keep up on the 2nd day into the race.

On the third day the race we crossed into the GREAT State of Kansas, and I emphasize GREAT as a sense of extreme exaggeration. It happened to be my turn on the bike and I remember thinking, 'this can't be too bad. At least it's flat,' a novice cyclist's dream. But after several hours, the cross winds and quarter head winds started to impact the team, and we were some exhausted cyclists. So,

I was riding and wore out and tired of Kansas when I found myself on a 4-lane highway. I was on the shoulder of the far right lane when a significant gust of wind came up just as I was crossing a railroad track. Wind and railroad tracks are not a good combination for cyclists, and my front tire was suddenly caught in the track. It happened so fast, I was unable to unclip my prosthetic leg from my pedal.

I'd been on the bike for 30 minutes or so prior to this, and my residual limb was significantly slippery with sweat. When I attempted to unclip my foot, my residual limb slid directly out of the prosthetic and it was left still attached to the bike. Now, the bike holding my prosthetic was laying on the road over there, and I, without it, was laying on the road over here, while a semi-truck in the adjacent lane was traveling in the same direction. I heard the truck engage its jake brakes, and I was laying in the road thinking, 'I can survive a 155m antitank improvised explosive device in Iraq, but I am going to be run over by a semi in Kansas while riding a bike in a safe country instead of in combat?' It just didn't make sense! How was my family going to explain this? Mason can go through and survive 34 different surgeries, 3 -1/2 months bedridden, 18 months wheelchair-bound, metal in his neck, back, left leg and an amputation of the right leg below the knee -- and then he was killed riding a bike in <u>Kansas?</u>

Luckily, I was not hit by the semi-truck, but it's hard not to imagine what the driver was thinking when he saw a one-legged man flying off his bike for no apparent reason. Fortunately, the vehicle behind me stopped and asked if I needed assistance, and I did not hesitate to ask for it, unlike in most cases. They gave me a towel, and I dried my residual limb off, put my prosthetic leg back on, straightened out my brake and gear levers, and finished my shift until the next racer took over. So, this is how I got my RAAM tattoo, the first time I had ever fallen off my bike while on the move. I suffered road rash on my right arm below my elbow as well as on my right thigh, where the "tattoo" is with me today. A few days later we crossed the finish line in Annapolis, MD and were the first American team consisting of wounded veterans. Team 4 Mil's Warrior 8-man team crossed the country in 7 days, 2 hours and 50 minutes."

My first road trip across Kansas took place at the end of my freshman year in college. I'd flown west to attend classes at the California School of Fine Arts in San Francisco, and at the end of the summer, I impulsively bought a pan head Harley Davidson for $100 and set out at midnight for home in Pennsylvania. Of course, I had no idea I'd be cycling across Kansas 51 years later, but I did reveal my aptitude for 2-wheeled marathons by riding the first 450 miles to Winnemucca, NV, in one sitting on an implausibly loud, slow, brutish machine, wearing no goggles or helmet. Following Rte 40 and what would later become I-80, I rode east through Utah and crossed the Rockies at Rabbit Ears Pass in a hailstorm. The Harley's electricals were not accustomed to moisture, and I had to coast the last few miles down the eastern slope, where, after some uninspired haggling at a gas station, I gladly sold the hog for $35.

After a few hours sleep in a $7 motel room, I hitched a ride with a taciturn rancher in a 1946 Chevrolet sedan. We drove into a constant headwind all the way from Colorado to Manhattan, KS, and averaged about 2 spoken words per mile. My second ride was in a small refrigerated truck hauling fish to Kansas City. The driver was openly contemptuous of my artsy-fartsy summer indulgence and lectured me on the benefits of learning a manly trade, like driving a truck. I was too grateful for the ride to argue his case, which anyway made some sense, but his attitude towards me changed after a sudden blow-out threatened to tumble us down a steep embankment. I was exhausted enough to calmly accept an early death, while the terrified driver wrestled with the swerving truck and brought it to a halt inches from the precipice. As he sat paralyzed with fear, hyper-ventilating, white knuckles glued to the steering wheel, I got out, found the jack and changed the tire just as I'd done dozens of times growing up on a farm. In fact, we had an identical truck body minus the reefer in the bed. Back on the road again, I was too tired to think much about what might have happened. When we got to Kansas City, he pulled a wad of cash from his wallet and insisted I take it. I declined, thanked him for the ride and hitched the rest of the way home, grateful for art school, for growing up on in the country, and for finding someone in Colorado who would pay me $35 cash for that miserable, pan head Harley.

Sometime after midnight, east of Maize, Kansas, just north of Wichita, we're pulled off the side of the road preparing for Dur to come in. Looking westward, we see what must be the lights of Dur's follow van coming our way. We've learned that distances on the plains are deceiving, and if he appears to be 5 minutes away, it's more likely 10. Taylor has my TT bike ready to go, and as usual, we stand around waiting, but we're all too tired to say much and we let the crickets and cicadas do the talking for us. Their *chirring* sound is soothingly welcome. It plays like a healing vibration, a hymn to stillness, a symphonic orchestra of insects playing a benefit concert just for us. Then a big rig roars by heading east, and all is momentarily lost in its bellowing diesel bawl. But when the noise abates, the *chirring* concert gradually returns, and I notice the wind has finally declared a truce. I can hear the world around me and for the first time in six wind-blown hours, and I remember what it's like to relax.

Maybe the crickets and cicadas have rejuvenated Chris and Taylor, too, because this is the time and place where we establish a tradition we will re-enact throughout the rest of the RAAM. Its rules are to be found nowhere in any of the RAAM manuals, but it goes exactly like this: When you're all prepared and waiting for the exchange with the incoming rider, you throw stones at stuff. It's easy: bend down, scrabble in the roadside litter for a rock, stand back up and pick a target. Fence posts, road signs, guard rails, tree trunks, abandoned metal mail boxes -- anything is fair game. Fire away, and you get extra points for the loudest rock/target impact. The genius of this mindless act is that it's stupidly relaxing. Our extreme team ambition to leave a high mark in the RAAM record book needs to be remembered with every pedal stroke, while this chucking of rocks needs no skill, no discipline, no memory, no recording of hits and misses, no effort at all but the exercise of dumb fun, which in this case, is smart. Compared with the intense focus on a definitive goal, the aimlessness of aiming at nothing is subversively appealing. Whenever I think of Chris, Taylor and Nate, I'll remember this important, improbable ritual.

Dur and I end our shift at 1:30 in the morning in El Dorado, KS. We've covered 170 miles in more than 9 hours, and thanks to the wind letting up in Maize, our average speed since we left Ford came back up close to 18 mph, not bad considering the roads and breezy weather. Michael and Dave take off into the dark of night while Dur and I have a quick Manny-meal, a shower and a massage. Our neck muscles are hurting badly, and despite Lydia's skill, the painful aftermath of those segmented road bumps lingers on. An hour later, as the RV speeds eastward, we're sound asleep when we finally do Get the Hell Out of Dodge, and I'm not sorry I wasn't awake to say good bye to Kansas -- *state mammal the Bison, state bird the meadowlark, state amphibian the barred salamander, which can grow to 14 inches long !*

From west of the Colorado/Kansas border all the way to El Dorado, KS, we have been on a portion of the vast Ogallala aquifer which lies 200 to 400 ft below us. This ancient, shallow, 8-state reservoir stretches from Nebraska to Texas and provides almost a third of the nation's water used for agriculture. The water sequestered here is not made up of last weeks' rain water seeping into the ground; it is ancient *paleo*water slowly accumulated during the Pliocene era and the last ice age, 10,000 years ago. This enormous resource has made these former dustbowl states agriculturally viable, and yet, the millions of gallons of water drawn from it every year since the 1940s far exceeds the rate of replenishment. It's expected the aquifer will be pumped dry by the middle of this century.

The currently infamous Keystone pipeline crosses the Ogallala aquifer near our team exchange in El Dorado, just east of Wichita. The conflicting opinions concerning the mixing of oil and water are beyond discussion here, but the RAAM's journey through a diversity of physical landscapes and political beliefs does create a rich context within which our 4 tiny racer-dots are moving across a seemingly one-dimensional map. For me, it's at intersections such as this confluence of a modern pipeline and an ancient aquifer that a greater picture emerges. Every crossing of a border line, a river or a mountain is likely to be accompanied by a change in our physical and mental landscapes. The boundaries of our energies at these crossings are sometimes driven by the environment, sometimes distracted by thoughts originating across other boundaries. For me, we are navigating more than just secondary highways; we are navigating a *self* through a set of circumstances that sometimes mix no better than oil and water. Riding across this complicated country with all its natural beauties and disparate cultural contradictions is informed by not only *where* we are, but also by *who* we are, and how the RAAM will intersect with who we will become.

And it's with this thought that I must face one of those ironies that turns an otherwise consistent principle upside down, and tempers my haste to judge others whose principles conflict with what I *believe* to be mine (not that I'm particularly adroit at following my own counsel). Politically, I fall into the category of tree-hugging, re-cycling, liberal-leaning, climate change alarmists. I deplore malls and the wretched excess of unbridled consumerism, and I applaud the development of energy sources which eliminate the burning of fossil fuels. My team mates and I may be riding across the country powered by whole wheat pasta and pedals, but before I get all huffy about the Canadian shale oil pipeline, I need to 'fess up to an immense paradox. The carbon footprint left by our 5 support vehicles, x 3,000 miles -- not to mention the air miles accumulated by the crew and team, plus the friends and families flown to and from the RAAM's beginning and end -- forever rescind my right to be *holier-than-thou* when it comes to "protecting the environment."

We wake up around 9:00 in the morning along Highway 54, some 40+ miles into Missouri. It's a relief to see lush, green grass and leafy maples, oak and ash trees, typical of what we'll be riding through from now on. Our little land-borne armada is docked next to a convenience store which appears to be the community hub, with cars and trucks constantly pulling in and out. It's a lot easier to picture a tiny town in Missouri as a church-supper, white-picket-fence, Norman Rockwell community than it is to picture it as a place where people are buying and selling drugs, but that's exactly what they're doing here on Main Street in middle-America. Both Taylor and Lewis witness some brisk business transactions in a car parked nearby. The evidence is so graphic that Taylor calls 911, and within minutes, he and the occupants of the car are interviewed by the men in blue.

The Missouri climate is the first we've had with temperatures in the 90s mixed with equally high humidity. "Sweating like a pig" is a tempting way to describe how we feel, but it's a misleading term; pigs perspire only through their snouts, just as dogs utilize only their tongues. We humans have sweat glands over most of our bodies, and in Missouri, we human cyclists are sweating not *like*, but, *worse* than pigs. When the ambient air is dry, perspiration helps keep body temperatures down due to the effects of evaporative cooling. Hot, humid conditions give no such relief, and the body expends huge amounts of energy and fluids to keep core temperatures at safe levels, which means less energy is available for turning the pedals. With this in mind, crew chief Dave passes out cold packs and 'do rags to the racers. We keep them on ice in the racer van food chest. Each time I get back in the van, I take my helmet off, aim the AC vent at my face, put a cold 'do rag on my head and stuff a cold pack down the front and back of my jersey. Ten or fifteen minutes is plenty of cool-off time to offset the heat we soak up while we ride through Camdenton towards Missouri's state capital, Jefferson City.

The route is an easy series of rolling hills through pretty countryside, good pavement and minimal traffic, so that over the next 100 miles we're able to average a respectable 20 mph, despite the heat and aching necks. After the hardships

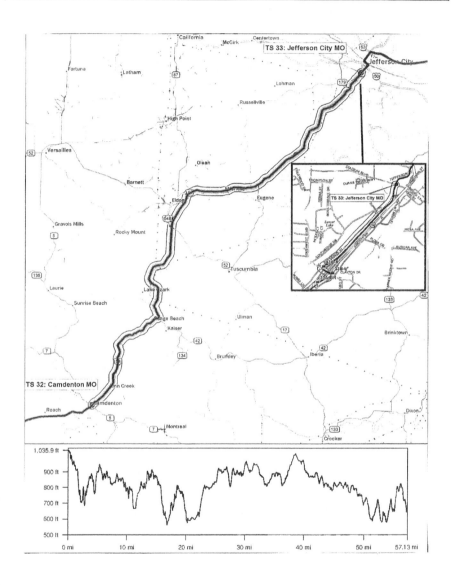

of Kansas, it seems we've found the pop sports-culture equivalent of a "second wind." Whatever its name, it's a welcome guest in the House of Hurt we've come to occupy.

Once we're in Jefferson City, the pace slows down, the streets are congested and the racer van can't find an opportunity to pass Dur, so we get to watch him sprint away from green lights and wind his way up the hill to the grand, neo-classical, dome-topped Capitol Building that stands high above the city. Dur is undoubtedly frustrated by the traffic, but we applaud like a quiz show audience as he rides wicked-fast (and legally) through all the downtown obstacles.

We exchange riders north of the city and I experience the first of several on-ramp, off-ramp nightmares we'll encounter half-a-dozen times as we ride into increasingly populated areas. Some of these intersections are wide, multi-laned mazes, and appear to attract texting teenagers and half-blind seniors driving as if *they're* the ones racing across America. The worst combination happens when I'm hugging the right shoulder of a 3-lane highway, and there's traffic entering from the on-ramp to the right. I simultaneously need to negotiate safe passage between these on-ramp vehicles -- all eager to assassinate me -- before I somehow cross the 3 lanes on my left, which can mean threading through menacing traffic going 3 times my speed -- in order to make a left-hand turn a half-mile away. There are no other situations on the RAAM in which I feel so paranoid, so out-of-place, so vulnerable. Bike skills, fitness, speed and savvy mean nothing here; these big highway intersections are a RAAMracer's worst nightmare.

I survive the murderous Jefferson City intersection, cross the bridge over the Missouri River, turn east, and am blessed with a sweet little tailwind. Dur and I trade off a few times, average over 20 mph, and end our day at the team exchange around suppertime in Mokane, Mo, pop. 185. We barely see Michael and Dave during the frantic swapping of coolers, bikes and equipment, but they seem strong and steady, and off they go. Our RVs are parked in the shade of a couple of giant cottonwoods on the edge of a ball field, which has a storage shed with flush toilet bathrooms. (Brilliant choice of sites, crew chief Dave!) Dur gets on the massage table while I change out of my damp, nasty shorts and jersey and get into the portable shower set up next to the RV.

Howard Conway

"A few days from the start, I took on the job of getting the temporary shower set up like Lewis taught me. I gathered, towels, soap, shoes, had the water hot, nothing left to chance, everything ready. It was a fun job as the racers appreciated it and they become thankful of not having to shower in the RV. At one point, Dur didn't want to dry off in the damp wet shower tent, so he just walked out naked. I reminded him there were people around, and he said, 'Who wants to see a naked, 70-year old man?' and just proceeded to dry himself off. Don and Michael really enjoyed the outdoor shower and I tried to treat them special. Another time, we were parked close to a gas station and convenience store. When Michael finished his shower, I had a shirt for him and he put it on and wrapped a towel around his waist and walked over and went in the store with just the shirt and towel on. Really a funny sight, he was so damn skinny it seemed the towel wrapped around him twice. I would like to have seen the people's faces in the store when they got in line behind him and the clerk took his money. But nudity was no big deal to these guys. They'd walk over to the massage table with only a towel on and lay down on the table in the

middle of small towns and get their massages. It was sort of like a hospital. No modesty became the routine and it made the racers seem more real."

What a pleasure it is to smell *good* for a change, even better to smell just a bit like my wife I've been missing so much. I can't thank the crew enough for this simple luxury. After much too long for anyone but a teenager, I leave the shower wrapped in a soft terry cloth towel and trade places with Dur on Lydia's massage table. She tends to my neck and the tight hamstring that cramped outside of Flagstaff, and, within a few minutes, I am thoroughly, light-headedly, Jack Daniels *relaxed.* The exhaustion accumulated over the last 8 hours is being replaced with the sedatives of soap and water, clean clothes and a massage. All I need now is a big bowl of Manny's spaghetti and a 4-hour nap and I'll be back to believing the RAAM is still the greatest adventure ever.

Lydia Brewster

"Every time I've challenged myself to recall just why I agreed to join the RAAM team I have come up with a different conclusion. It is true that my youngest daughter's disapproval of my disinclination to spend over a week with a bunch of obsessive men who actually care deeply about winning a bicycle race that most people have never heard of made me feel what I have so often felt in my life: unadventurous. My penchant for being self-critical reared up and, in a brief moment of bravura, I agreed to join the team. At the time, fall or winter I am not sure, June seemed so far away. Surely some quirk of fate or circumstance might happen that would cancel the trip; the riders after all were getting long in the tooth. It seemed possible that one of them would develop a bum knee, a heart condition, or something that would prevent the foursome from continuing

126

*with their quest. Having ministered to Michael Patterson's
bicycle-related wounds over many years, it seemed likely
that at least another medical emergency would become an
issue over the next few months.*

*It was on the first conference call that I knew I was
not RAAM material. Dave Eldridge commanded the call
in what felt like military style, all competence, strategy,
tactics, and terms that were meaningless to me. It was as
if I had suddenly joined the wrong meeting (I have done
this), realizing too late that I was supposed to be with the
group in Room 210. But, alas, it was too late to excuse
myself. How could it be that grown men would be fretting
about their bicycle togs? Staring at the spread sheet on
my kitchen counter as I listened, helplessly, to the banter
among the group I feared the worst; how could I have been
such a fool, needing a vacation as much as I did, to have
signed on to travel with intense competitors, techies, and a
military commander!*

*Deeper than the challenge to my cautious nature,
though, was the tempting opportunity to give up all
choice (almost) and confront my many small and large
phobias. I wanted to be uncomfortable again as I had
been on a life-changing trip to Nepal when the goal was
to survive, adapt, and find joy in small things. There
have only been a few times in my life when I have had
no choices and in each of those circumstances I have
found it profoundly stimulating to manage, even survive,
with inner resources I rarely use. That a shower can be
so meaningful can put all else in its proper perspective.
Out of my element, careening down mountain passes,
forced to trust someone I don't know at the wheel,
frightened out of my wits I found it thrilling to give up
the control I usually command. The appointed truck stop
or abandoned gas station was perhaps more an oasis to*

me than to others with fewer inner demons. Still alive, I performed my duties and awaited the next leg of hell on wheels. Ashamed as I am of my fear of speed and speed in vehicles in particular, it was my small RAAM victory to have endured the colossal lack of control that I encountered in our rank-smelling RV.

But, more basic than my inner challenges was a real feeling of loyalty to Michael and Elena Patterson. Their love of cycling, his determination to succeed, and their many kindnesses to me over a long period of time made my decision easier. Down deep I wanted to be a part of Michael's dream team and was flattered to be included.

I had fully expected to follow Dave's master plan to shift from one RV to the other on regular intervals. I shall forever be grateful to Dave for pretending not to notice my insubordination when I moved into the RV driven by Barney and Michael on a semi-permanent basis. My nerves had their limits and while Lewis and Howard were charming in most every way, their driving styles were not going to work for me; Barney and Michael, perhaps sensing my insecurity, drove with a less NASCAR-ish style. Howard sweetly apologized for scaring me and acknowledged he liked to drive fast. Lewis liked to be in the lead, demonstrating this with a U-turn complete with squealing tires. I sensed that Lewis was much more like my own husband and would have eventually tired of humoring me and urged me to shut up and go to sleep (an impossibility) if his driving bothered me.

Sleep was the challenge for everyone. I believe each member of the crew worked hard to cope with its lack and developed tricks to survive on little. Oddly, although I still wonder if I actually slept at all, I did not feel as exhausted as I should have, until the end when I settled into my bed in Annapolis and slept as if dead. Don's generosity to share some of his Ambien saved me from coming apart at the seams; four hours of semi-sleep refreshed me. I made peace early on that I would be too nervous to sleep while climbing or descending mountainsides. I felt that my inherent nervousness might come in handy when our exhausted drivers might need to be roused. I learned to move my frame around rather efficiently in my bench-seat-bed, even extending my heels onto the cot on the other side of the RV to allow me to stretch out. I think everyone tried the rear berth and, except for Dur, rejected it when they found it similar to being stapled to the tail of a fish.

Navigating was an acquired skill. Having lost my map reading skills to a dependence upon Google maps, I struggled to keep my driver adequately informed. Both Barney and Michael showed great patience with my ineptitude and covered for my mistakes. The route book's long narrative style was the sleep aid I really responded to, and on several occasions, I found myself jerking awake in shame. I improved over time, but only modestly.

I did not believe Karen's prediction that we would all acquiesce to eating junk food, but she was right. The effort to eat much else seemed too much to expend. I still remember fondly savoring two Snickers ice cream bars in Arizona at one of many stops during which we attempted unsuccessfully to regroup and make plans with the other RV. Small pleasures of all sorts become important when the main order of the day is persevering. Near the end of the race, while waiting anxiously for Michael and Dave to emerge from the last, long leg, I enjoyed a Fillet-o-Fish sandwich, and then, throwing caution to the wind, knowing it was nearly over, I ate another. Who knew one could celebrate on a MacDonald's menu item?

The landscape was thrilling to me. I once drove across the country in a Honda box van full of motocross bikes, *and this trip reminded me of that memory. I am lamely content to pass through the world wondering who lives in the houses I pass. On this trip I found myself settling into those thoughts and imaginings. I was stunned by the harshness of the Kansas crossing and found myself asking a clerk in one of the restaurants we visited what brought her to there? She said if it weren't for family ties she would leave in a second; the constant wind had gotten to her as it had to us on that day.*

The moonscape through Arizona felt all wrong, as if we were travelers in a Sam Shepherd play or visiting a strange planet. I felt a melancholy settle over me as I stared out at the little lonely settlements and unforgiving ground. My New England blood can barely fathom that much space with so little sign of encouragement beyond oversized neon signs against the backdrop of sky, wind, and dry heat. I was glad to leave that place. Ohio's little winding roads through farms and small towns, on the other hand, looked so much more beautiful than on other visits. I was glad for the circuitous route book here taking us to places you would never see on an interstate. The place my memory has returned to again and again is the lovely little town in Colorado on the other side of the mountains. Having a hurried meal in a pretty little downtown restaurant was the only time on the trip when I longed for a glass of wine. I was glad to discover that my nightly glass of wine did not have the same appeal at a truck stop.

The team and crew turned out to be a big surprise. I thoroughly enjoyed them and had some very meaningful conversations with a number of them in rare and remarkable moments over a cheeseburger or while stowing gear. It was very enlightening and stimulating to feel a sense of family with a group who mostly did not share my perspectives or my politics. On only a few occasions did talk veer into the out-of-bounds zone of maligning certain political leaders, and on at least one occasion, I reminded the group that we were a team of many different stripes. Everyone seemed to accept that our individual lifestyles or beliefs were secondary to being the best team and crew possible. It was remarkably military in many, many ways.

I was challenged to care about winning and meeting our goal as I understood that was essential if we were to be a team. Even as I fulfilled my role and tried to be useful in as many ways as I was able, I found myself still more of an observer. I am a remote person by nature, so to live communally with RAAM's diverse group was challenging and thrilling. Manny, Michael Scholl, and others warned those of us new to RAAM that there would likely be friction among the team. Tales of mutinous RAAM teams of the past cast an ominous foreboding of fireworks to come. While there were some schoolboy jabs and teasing that sometimes felt as though they crossed a line, there seemed, in general, to be geniality and respect among the group. Perhaps newcomers that had nothing to do with the sport like Janice and myself were eyed with caution but, if so, I did not sense it. I was relieved that I seemed to rank well against one notorious massage therapist from a previous RAAM who was described to me by Manny as intolerable.

The book I brought along -- about a Boston native who owns a haberdashery but decides in late middle age to return to a remote part of Africa he experienced as a young man -- was my salvation. Accompanying the main character on his harrowing journey was my companion on the RAAM; somehow I managed to totally escape my terrors every time I returned to the page. His plight was so much more terrifying than mine. I would never go anywhere without a good book.

Would I ever consider doing anything like this again? No. It was a very difficult week. Yet the trip was exactly what I expected it to be, and what I hoped it would be: I was pushed well beyond my comfort zone and, strangely, I feel that I can check off another item on my need for a little adventure list. A friend who sat beside me on a rickety bus on one-lane switchbacks in the Himalayas said, 'If we go over the edge, at least our children will have the fun of telling a great story about how we died; we will have spared them the misery of having us plugged into a glucose machine without our teeth!' Adventures are not, by definition, always fun, but they are necessary."

"If you didn't know your age, what age would you be?"

Satchel Paige

DAY FIVE
Mokane, MO to McArthur, OH
613 miles

Missing-What-You-Thought-You'd-See is one of the signature ironies of the RAAM. Monument Valley, Wolf Creek Pass, the mighty Mississippi and Gettysburg would, in my mind, become the memorable markers of my cycling experience, a Cliff Notes course on Americana as seen from under a bike helmet. The problem is that all these iconic milestones fall into Michael and Dave's rotations. Except for Wolf Creek Pass, the riding is at night: they don't get to see them either.

Tonight, for instance Michael and Dave cross the Missouri River on the Lewis Bridge, named after Meriwether Lewis, and a few miles later, they'll cross the Mississippi into Alton, Illinois on the Clark Bridge, named for William Clark. Both bridges are memorials to the Lewis and Clark expedition of 1804-1806, whose exploration of the northern reaches of the Louisiana Purchase began here at the confluence of the Missouri, the Illinois and Mississippi Rivers. The 1928, 2-lane version of the Clark Bridge was expanded in 1994 to 4 lanes and 2 bike paths. In 1993, still under construction, it survived the worst flood in modern history, with waters 20 feet above flood stage level at St. Louis. I'm familiar with some of this history only because my friend Neil Goodwin made a documentary film of the bridge during the long course of its construction. The film was shown on NOVA in 1997 and is terrific, so I wish I could go back home and tell Neil I'd ridden over his bridge, but only Michael or Dave could do that now. Alton was also the site of two crucial events leading up to the Civil

War. In 1837, a pro-slavery mob from Kansas killed the abolitionist printer and Reverend, Elijah Lovejoy, and threw his printing presses into the Mississippi. In 1858, the 7th debate between the pro-slavery Douglas and the abolitionist Lincoln was held in Alton in front of 6,000 spectators, and paved the way to Lincoln's presidency in 1860. Musician Miles Davis, MLK assassin James Earl Ray and Robert Wadlow, the world's tallest human at 8 ft, 11 inches, were all born in Alton. How much of this Michael or Dave are aware of as they ride across the Clark Bridge is a lot more than Dur and I are aware of, sound asleep as we are in the racers' RV.

Nate Keck

"The fatigue of the previous 4 days is starting to show. Crewmembers are becoming more easily agitated and the racers don't have the same pep and enthusiasm they had at the start of the race. I have heard it said that it is times like this that 'champions are made', and I'm thinking it may well be true as the team and the crew tries to rally itself for the final push to the finish."

Just south of Alton, St. Louis is the biggest metropolitan area along our entire route. In order to avoid Interstate 270, Michael and Dave's crossing at Alton is accompanied as usual by the follow van and the racer van. Meanwhile, the 2 RVs and crew chief Dave's van take Interstate 270 around St. Louis on the most direct route to our next rider exchange in Alhambra, Il. Our convoy is led by the crew RV, driven and navigated by Lewis and Howard, followed by the racer RV, driven and navigated by Michael Scholl and Barney. Last in line are crew chief Dave and Karen in Dave's van. As Dave recalls, there were about a dozen vehicles between him and the racer RV. He can see the lights on the back of the RV, but with the exchange point 100 miles away, he feels no need to stay tightly grouped in this Wednesday evening traffic.

As the convoy starts up a ramp onto the highway, Dave sees something flying through the air somewhere behind the RV. Karen excitedly exclaims, "*It's a bicycle!*" and as traffic moves towards it at 50 mph, they are horrified to think that a cyclist riding up the on-ramp was hit, and was possibly being run over at this moment. Dave knows it can't be Michael or Dave Burnett, but he flips on his hazard lights and cautiously slows down. Cars are bunching up behind him, and now he sees the bike lying half in the ramp lane, half in the grass triangle between the ramp and the highway. It appears to be still in one piece, but there is no rider in sight. In the next instant, his headlights catch the familiar, reflective tape on the bicycle's wheels, and under the seat, the unique, rectangular rider number issued by the RAAM.

Because of the traffic, Dave isn't able to pull off the road safely for another 100 yards up the hill. As he rushes back along the curbside grass to retrieve the bike, he's aware that cars coming up the ramp can't see the bike until the last moment, and when they do finally see it, they swerve to the right and seem to miss it -- or not; he can't believe they'll *all* miss it. What he knows for certain is that when a vehicle runs over a carbon-fiber frame, it will shatter into a thousand pieces. Running along the unlit ramp, out of breath, heart pounding, Dave dreads finding the mess he's so sure he will find.

Michael Scholl and Barney, by now, are a few miles farther down the road with Michael at the wheel of the racer RV. As usual, the NASCAR crew RV is well ahead of them. I'm in the bunk above the racer RV cab and Dur is zoned out in the springboard "master suite" at the rear.

Traffic is moving along briskly on three lanes, so Michael is startled when a pickup truck pulls in much too close to his driver's-side window. He steers to the right to avoid a scrape, but the pickup stays parallel with him and the guy leaning halfway out the passenger-side window is shouting and gesturing towards the back of the RV. "A bike fell off!" he yells, "A bike fell off"!

Michael and Barney are in shock: it's a nightmare, the worst. Of all things to happen, it had to happen within their purview. As Michael pulls over onto the breakdown lane, his cell phone rings: it's Dave Eldridge.

I'm still floating in Ambien heaven with my Bose ear phones on, out cold in the bunk above the cab. As always, the crew lets us sleep until an hour or so before the rider exchange, which is scheduled for 1 in the morning. Around midnight, I feel the familiar tug on my foot, and I ask, *"Are we still in Kansas, Toto?"*

Howard Conway

"In all my years of involvement in sports, I learned that many seasons, practices, games and tournaments were apt to have a 'defining moment', a single incident that defined how the event went, good or bad, bonded the team together or pulled it apart. Like when Larry Bird dived for a loose ball in the championship game against the Lakers and it made all the other Celtics want to play harder, and it gave them the edge. Or when Ray Lewis would make that spectacular stop head-on against a running back, sacrificing his body for the good of the team. Or maybe when a great team is assembled with many personalities and they cannot get the chemistry right, it takes a defining moment to pull it all together, much like this year's LA Lakers basketball team. Sometimes it was at practice when the coach said something that really moved everyone to play better. You just never knew when the

defining moment was going to happen. What I will call our defining moment came in Illinois when Don's TT bike flew off the back of the racer RV.

All we knew from a phone call was that Dave had picked Don's bike up off the highway and we were all stopping so he could bring it up and put it back on the racer RV bike rack. The question about how in hell that could have happened was all we could talk about. This was a potentially divisive event between the racers and crew, and we were all extremely anxious about how it would go. When they woke Don up and told him what had happened, he just smiled and said, 'No problem, guys. I never liked that damn bike anyway.'"

The big picture is immediately easy to draw, even if I'm still half asleep. First of all, this crew is the best bunch of competent, hard working people any RAAM racer could ever ask for. Secondly, we have a total of 8 bikes and 4 or 5 sets of spare wheels. If we're down to 7 bikes for 4 riders, so what? We're still ridiculously over-equipped to finish the last third of the race. This little mishap is not so much a problem about an injured bicycle as it is an opportunity to heal some injured feelings, and it's made easy for me because I'm more a bike slob than a bike snob (just ask Kayla). For me, racing bikes are replaceable, occasionally annoying tools that cost much too much, but are nonetheless essential. Among my teammates, I'm by far the least attached to my bikes -- especially this TT. My legs like it, but my neck hates it. So, I'm especially glad it wasn't one of my teammates' cherished bikes, and I want the crew to feel at least as comfortable as I do. When Taylor says the bike can be easily repaired, I answer, "You mean I have to keep riding that goddamned thing?"

Howard Conway

"This was our defining moment. Why? Because the crew felt so bad and was so upset, thinking who was at fault, what would Don's reaction be, and Don defused it. He just as easily could have placed blame on people and blew a gasket but he didn't. We were lucky it was Don's bike. I won't say any more about that, but I can tell you right here and now, every crew member from then on would do anything for Don. It was the perfect reaction for what happened, and it drove the Racers and the Crew together like a nail in wood. The tension that had built up seemed to melt away and from then on everyone was just working hard together to get to the end."

As for figuring out how the bike got loose, I feel awful for whoever might think it was his/her fault and I'm totally sympathetic to how it might have happened. With roughly 140 transfers on and off the bike racks every 24 hours for 6-1/2 days, there are over 900 opportunities for error, one every 20 minutes or so. There are 2 crucial moves required of each transfer: swinging open or shut a bar that stabilizes the front wheel, and ratcheting tight, or opening up, a strap securing the rear wheel to the tray channel. Getting the bikes on and off the rack extra-quickly is sometimes essential, sometimes alongside fast moving roadside traffic. A third of these bike transfers are done in the dark, and except for Day One, they are all done under the added stress of exhaustion. *Nine hundred transfers?!* It's a miracle that a lot more bikes didn't take flight a lot more often.

Damage report? The front tubular tire is shredded, but the carbon wheel is surprisingly round and true. The rear wheel is also perfect, which is a relief, as each wheel costs north of $1,000. There's an inconsequential scrape mark on the outboard end of the left handlebar, a little scuff on the left side of the seat and another rasp across the left end of the rear-wheel skewer. Most interesting, the left Speedplay pedal has about a quarter of an inch ground off its outer perimeter. What remains is so perfectly machined that the shape looks intentional, and as I soon discover, the pedal continues to function flawlessly. There is no visible damage to the right side of the bike whatsoever. Taylor gets my spare front wheel from the van and within minutes, the TT is ready to ride, despite my hopes to the contrary.

It's 12:50 a.m., Thursday, June 21st in Alhambra, IL. Dur and I are waiting in the humid night air, ready for the team exchange. Michael and Dave come in on time having averaged over 19 mph since Mokane, MO. They seem, or attempt to seem, upbeat despite their conspicuous fatigue. I'm guessing we're all making an effort to keep our growing discomfort to ourselves. I know *I* am. As Michael passes by the follow-van's headlights, I notice he's stopped shaving, and I wonder if it's because he's too tired to bother, or because he's following the tradition of deer hunters and professional athletes who let their whiskers grow until they get their deer or win their championship. Michael and I are normally clean-shaven, but for these last few days Michael is apparently going back to the wild. I'm not sure his wife Elena would agree, but I think it looks good on him. The only reason I keep shaving is that I don't want to look even more derelict than I feel. I'm 2 years older than Michael and Dur, and 4 years older than Dave, *the kid*, so I cling to whatever pathetic vestiges of dignity I can muster. Both Dave and Dur sport beards year 'round, as do crew chief Dave, Barney, Ken, Howard and Michael Scholl. The rest of the guys are lately following Michael Patterson's approach, which will give the men on the team a bushy,

Grizzly-Adams, *"We-done-been-through-some-hellish-wild-territory"* credibility by the time we reach the swish comforts of Annapolis.

Our maps indicate Dur and I will be riding constant rollies most of the 165 miles to our next team exchange in Switz City, IN, pop. 293. If the rolling terrain is steep enough, the TT bike can stay on the bike rack and I can ride my comfy Scott roadie without wondering if my neck is going to snap in two. According to RAAM lore, we are about to enjoy the "easy" states, The Midwest Calm before The Appalachian Storm. Behind us, the ride across Kansas totaled close to 400 miles and lasted about 21 hours. Missouri was roughly 325 miles across and lasted 16 hours. Illinois, Indiana and Ohio will add up to only 500 miles *combined,* and take about 27 hours total. Going to sleep in one state and waking up in another will happen twice in this stretch, leading us all to the disorienting feeling of, *"Where the heck are we now?"*

Howard Conway

"Late at night in Ohio we were driving through a small town and the RV was smelling really bad. The water holding tank had not been emptied in several days and all the food prep and dish washing water from Manny's cooking was getting rank. People couldn't sleep, the smell was so overpowering. We didn't want to hunt for a place or stop, and Dave had told us not to dump water except in appropriate places, but it was difficult to find one this late at night. Eventually, we pulled off onto an empty lot of a vacant property covered with concrete. One of us ran out and pulled the lid off. The water drained out and we left the lid off the rest of the trip. The next day, Dave Eldridge was standing beside the RV when he saw a few drops of water on the ground under the tank. He asked someone

how the water got there. Must be a leak, was the innocent answer. No more questions, and no more wretched water smell in the RV."

Dur and I rotate 20-minute shifts as usual, but for the first time, he and I are dozing off the moment we're back in the racer van. The racer's seat is directly behind the passenger seat, cramped in against the coolers stacked behind the driver along with crates of drink supplements and bottles, alternate TT or road helmets, jackets, spare wheels and driver/navigator personal food and gear. Coach seating on a DELTA flight has about as much leg room. Additionally, our drivers/navigators are trying, justifiably, to stay awake and alert by playing music at considerable decibel levels, and the van is moving fast and bumpy to get to the next trade off. But we're so tired, none of that matters. For the first 4 days, I was never tempted to even close my eyes during these brief respites. But now, as the nighttime monotony wears on into the 4-in-the-morning dead zone, I gladly surrender. Futile as it may be to snooze for 5 minutes, I do, and immediately snap awake with a trickle of drool on my chin. These cat-nap, *kitten naps*, given their brevity, don't seem to be hurting our performance, but they do represent the beginning of a new generation of fatigue.

The coming of dawn gives us the usual energy boost, and as the daylight broadens, I stop the cat-naps. We're still passing signs for these little, back-road Illinois towns with little-town, mid-west names -- Newton, Willow Hill, Oblong, Robinson -- and the night-cooled air is redolent of damp, leafy woods, a welcoming, home-coming smell for me. There's very little traffic, thanks to the judicious planning by the RAAM organizers. Our speed is good, and now we're back to riding our TTs since the roads are smooth and not too hilly. These bikes are perfect for these conditions, and I apologize to mine for the grumpy remarks the night before. As if to accept my apology, Mr. Parlee takes me even faster over the last few miles to the Wabash River, which accounts for 130 miles since 1:30 in the morning back in Alhambra, all at an average of over 20 mph. *God bless America!*

Crossing the Wabash from Hutsonville, Illinois, into Graysville, Indiana, our clocks are turned ahead, and it's now 8:00 EST. How far could I be from the end if we've finally entered my native time zone? The question is best left rhetorical; better not to contemplate the 800 miles left or the endless little Indiana hills in front of us, but it still feels good to be *back east*. And so it goes, one mile at a time, pedal, pedal, pedal over the humpy 35 miles from the Wabash River to Switz City, where we swap the TTs in for our roadies. These hills are only 50-75 ft. high, but they come in dirty dozens, short and steep. For the first time, Dur looks as if he's hurting as much as I am, and I feel as if I'm slowing down, but I have no way to tell how much.

Yet another of the many topics we chewed over and over last winter was whether we should bring instrumentation to monitor our output of watts, heartbeat, cadence and speed. Weeks of debating Garmin-this, Polar-that, ended abruptly when we faced up to the obvious: 3 square inches of poorly lit plasma would be barely visible at night, and none of us could read the little numbers -- not to mention a restaurant menu, night *or* day -- without putting on our reading glasses. So, it became obvious we'd have to rely on *perception*. We trusted our years of experience would remind us of what it takes, for instance, to produce 220 watts for 20 minutes at a comfortable heart rate of 150. On a good training day, our perceptions will reasonably coincide with our instrumentation, but when acute fatigue is factored in, *perceived* effort becomes unreliable, and fatigue is having its way with us now.

I pedal into the morning sun while a crop duster flies low over corn fields to the north. This time, it's definitely not a UFO, although I still hold a tender memory for the one I so fervently believed I saw in Colorado. When I'm back in the racer van, Chris is talking excitedly about the plane. He loves flying anything with wings on it, and admits that the last house he bought was chosen because of its proximity to a small airfield, not that he mentioned it beforehand, he adds, to his loving wife.

Melinda Ashley

"When I met my husband, Don, 15 yrs ago, he mountain biked seriously, but did it purely for fun. He'd come home muddied and often bloodied, but his eyes would be dancing with excitement as he enthusiastically described the banter and camaraderie that was such a big part of the experience. His group referred to themselves as 'The Church of Our Lady of Perpetual Pedaling', a communion wine-drinking club with a biking problem. He was known as 'Padre Don.' They'd participate here and there in oddball races like 24-hr marathons where they'd ride steep single track loops on muddy, rocky terrain in the woods through the dark of the night and pouring rain. But his placement in these races was far less of a goal than was his simple enjoyment of being with his equally wacky cohorts, both male and female, whose ages ranged from age 14 up to however old Don was at the time, as he was always by far the oldest. I found not only the group spirit was wholesome and amazing, but each of the riders to be awe-inspiring and fun.

Because I was a professional artist raised in France among a family of musicians, the subject of sports rarely crossed my path, nor did sportsmen. Meeting Don when I was 45 was my first introduction to the world of 'sportifs'. My discovery of this new breed was all positive as I found their blissful enjoyment in jumping over brooks and logs as they tore thru the woods at high speeds, totally delightful. Don has always been an outdoorsman. He loves being in the woods and he knows every bump and turn on every trail within a wide radius from our home in New Hampshire. Second to riding the trails, his favorite thing in life is building them. He's probably built at least 20 miles just since I've known him. I loved watching him on a beautiful afternoon slink out his office door and disappear into the woods for hours with a chainsaw and loppers.

Then came the competitive racing. As Don became more interested in road cycling, and as he got more competitive and started to regularly climb the podium, the element of fun became less and less part of his narrative. The ride descriptions became less about the wise-cracks and banter exchanged, and more about the hardships of the ride and the long haul it took to get there and back. As the competitive element grew, his training got more and more serious. Summers were now 'racing season.' Vacation trips were cut short so as to not interrupt with his training. Spring became the prep for racing season and Don's rides became more specific in format. He now often turned down offers to ride with his buddies, couldn't go because he had to stick to his exacting training schedule. Gone were the days of simple, healthy exercise and camaraderie. Getting into racing moved his riding from pure fun to a job-like obligation, much more self-focused and driven by an increased ambition to win.

So, much of this new direction did not feel positive to me. His old biking passions were more than acceptable when he was having so much fun. My attitude was, 'more power to you.' But with the onset of competitive racing, not only was *it way less fun for him, I also felt a tinge of desperation. Because it went on for years, I felt determined to find a bright side to all of this, and I did find one. In comparison to Don's new, hyper-competitive racing pals, Don was only moderately obsessive. In hosting many of them in our home, I met some sweet, adorable people, but out there in a peloton, they were different animals, what I would call* scary *competitive. So compared to them, I could see that my Don was a comparatively relaxed and easy-going racer who could think about other things (momentarily at least!) One time, when I accompanied him for a week at one of the Senior Games events, we spent a good part of the week with other racers, mostly the scary types who are obsessively-well versed in exactly what to eat before, during and after a race. I was amused when we'd eat together at a restaurant and Don would let the others do the ordering first, and then say, 'I'll have what they're having.'*

The prospect of Don racing in the RAAM left me with a feeling of enduring dread. From the moment he was recruited, throughout the months of training, to the moment team T430 crossed the finish line, I had one desire, which was for RAAM to be over. There was very little about RAAM that made sense to me and no matter how I looked at it, it seemed that this race was less about cycling talent than about enduring agony. My greatest worry was about the lack of sleep and the bad judgment calls one makes during extreme exhaustion. My husband is a ridiculously light sleeper, so how well would he function after day 2 or day 3 or 4? What kind of mental acuteness could he possibly maintain?

I thought I'd perhaps find comfort in comparing the RAAM to the Tour de France, only to find that those riders enjoy a reasonable balance of recovery time vs. riding time, not to mention two days of total rest at the third-points of their (only) 2,000-mile route. Nor was it lost on me that the oldest post-war winner of the Tour, Cadel Evans, was 34 years old when he won in 2011. Put in perspective, Cadel is 12 years younger than Don's older daughter, and 37 years younger than Don. The amazing speeds and professionalism of Tour riders notwithstanding, when I considered the endurance challenges and extreme conditions that will be required of these 70-yr-old RAAMsters, it makes the Tour look not so tough.

While Don was gathering information about the RAAM, we watched a documentary about RAAM solo riders. One word wraps up my impression: 'Horrifying!' Don's initial reaction was not very different from mine, but a few days later, he began to rationalize away those images and say things like 'It's not the same thing with a team,' and, 'But I'm going to be careful, so this won't happen to me'. What stuck in my mind was the willingness of these racers to abuse themselves in their desperation to win, the extreme physical and mental torture they'd force upon the otherwise extremely healthy bodies they were blessed to possess. The legendary RAAM soloist, Jure Robic, described how stress had caused hallucinations, frightening paranoia and delirium. In an attempt to keep his mind active and legs pedaling, his accompanying crew shouted all sorts of insults and profanities at him, which succeeded in getting him to reply similarly back at them. He said since madness made the pain disappear and allowed him to continue, madness was the key to success.

My family has been stricken with several serious health tragedies which lead me to strenuously reject Robic's position. From my perspective, encouraging madness is an unforgivable madness in itself. Don has the damnedest good fortune to have the option to be in excellent health, and yet he was opting to put his enviable body thru unreasonable mistreatment for the purpose of -- winning a race? I just can't connect to that kind of thinking.

Through the months of training and prep for the RAAM I kept hoping to find something to take comfort from, and I found two things: the first was that our beloved country is not 5,000 miles across, and the second was when I heard Don's old pal Barney was going to be part of the crew. Upon learning this, I broke into tears of relief as I could not have wished for a more devoted, smart, competent, level-headed person to accompany Don on his journey; my guardian angel had arrived.

As the race plans took shape, I also became impressed by the size and competency of the crew, and this too assured me that even though it remained for me an insane event, at least it would be done in the best of hands. Don had nothing but praise for these generous souls, and I am grateful to each of them for their devotion and for taking personal time from their lives, and for the sacrifices they made in order to take such good care of my husband despite their pitiable lack of sleep, terrible food and gross living conditions.

And his team mates? I had heard all nice things about them as Don had met them several times, but until the rubber hits the road, it's not easy to know the nature of someone's character, temperament or level of maturity. What promises might these guys have made to themselves? How driven were they to win, and to what extent would they go to make it happen? Would any of them push themselves or their teammates too far? And what about the inevitable peer pressure, not necessarily the obvious, 'You must do as I do,' peer pressure, but the small inner voice that says in response, 'I don't want to be the slowest guy, I don't want to be a disappointment to the team.' Don was the oldest member of the team. Research shows that as age advances, every extra year brings with it the likelihood of a greater decline. Don was still setting personal bests into his 70s, so I wasn't so worried about an actual decline as I was about his pre-race determination to not let the team down."

On my second shift in Indiana, I spot a rider a mile in front of me, also headed eastward. It's surprising how rarely we've encountered local cyclists, so I'm curious, and like the typical, knuckleheaded predator-cyclist who can't resist chasing down innocent-prey cyclists, I push extra hard and slowly close the gap. Our fellow travelers, now reduced to the music-blaring *Spirit of Brazil, Georgia Chain Gang* and the recumbent *Team Bacchetta,* have traded places with us recently enough so I know it's not one of their riders. As I close the gap, a small camper with RAAM decals and caution blinkers passes with a friendly beep, and slows down behind the rider. I pedal closer and realize I've caught a soloist, one of the few we've seen, which also means he must be one of the last in place among those who have survived so far. (Of the 45 soloists who began the race, 28 officially finished. Some dropped out due to fatigue and some were disqualified for failing to meet certain time stations' minimums.)

When I ride up alongside him, he looks a lot better than I feel with his smooth pedal stroke, comfortable posture, big smile. We exchange encouragements, shrug off the immensity of our folly, and I ride on ahead feeling none of the competitive adrenaline boost that so often accompanies overtaking a rider on the road.

The fastest 2012 RAAM solo woman, Trix Zgraggen, is a 45-yr-old Swiss mother of four. She left Oceanside with the women soloists 4 days before us and will complete the race in 10 days, 13 hours and 39 minutes, arriving at the docks in Annapolis just minutes after we do. The fastest male soloist, Reto Schoch, 34, is also Swiss. His time of 8 days, 6 hours and 29 minutes, is the third fastest in the RAAM's history, with an average accumulated speed of 15.08 mph.

Our 4-man team's problems with fatigue are serious, but soloists have it 4 times worse. They are riding a race so much more grueling than ours that I almost feel guilty passing someone who has slept one quarter of the hours I've slept. For example, in order for solo winner, Reto Schoch, to finish the race in 8 days and 6 hours, he needs to pedal an average 364 miles every 24 hours. That's equivalent to the distance between San Diego, CA and Phoenix, AZ. Our 4-man team averages 458 miles every 24 hours, but that means an average of only 114.5 miles for each of us, *less than a third* of what he covers *by himself.* Assuming that Reto was off the bike, sleeping and eating for 3 hours out of each 24, he needed to average over 17 mph for the other 21 hours in order to achieve his accumulated average of 15.08 mph. On T430, we were each on the bike racing an average of 6 hours out of every 24, and there were no hours during which one of the team wasn't on the road, unlike the solo riders. When they stop to sleep, their race clocks keep ticking. During his entire 8.25 day RAAM, Reto slept a total of approximately 16-18 hours and pedaled 184-186 hours out of a little over 200 hours. We've all at some point in our lives had a week with very little sleep, but combining the lack of sleep with pedaling a bicycle during every waking hour is another order of magnitude. Over the course of our 6.55 day RAAM, each of us slept maybe 39 hours and pedaled about 39 hours. The difference between our average speed of 19.04 mph and Schoch's 15.08 average seems amazingly small considering he rode all the hours and miles by himself. It's these soloists' performance that tempers my pride when I'm congratulated on the RAAM ride. I want to protest -- and usually do -- that compared to the soloists, we were just out for a long Sunday ride.

We're 30 miles east of the Wabash, and the clip on my left shoe is beginning to fail. I spend 5-10 seconds riding at the start of each pull before getting my shoe locked securely into the pedal. The Speedplay shoe clip is designed around a simple spring-wire that can fail to engage if a bit of road crud jams it's movement. Clearing it out with a paper clip or safety pin is all it usually takes to free it up, an easy remedy that takes a minute or two, but it doesn't occur to me to fix it, or ask Taylor to fix it. This pesky clip is not so much an impediment to speed as it is a reminder of Murphy's Law. I place it under the big tent of, *"Shit happens,"* and the reason I put up with it goes like this: I'm convinced we are going to make it to Annapolis, but within that certainty is also a belief that it's meant to cost. There's no free lunch. I am, therefore, by this fatigue-induced reasoning, somehow *obligated* to endure a measure of discomfort in exchange for the reward. By some further, clever realignment of logic, I allow myself to assign equal value to the wide range of obstacles that could stop us, from cardiac arrest to a mosquito bite. I'm convinced we are due a finite number of obstacles, no more, no less, but finite. Having such a minor obstacle as a jammed shoe clip is a credit voucher and brings me closer to my quota with trivial consequences. Such are the curious workings of RAAMbrain two-thirds through the race.

As if to confirm my finite-quota-of-obstacles theory, I'm ambushed by a small brown bird. It happens so fast that I can't identify the bird or know if it survived, but I do sense it coming at me from the left side, auguring its beak into my forearm and continuing in tumbling flight off to my right in a flurry of feathers. The little triangular flap of skin halfway between my wrist and elbow seeps a tattoo of blood, but it's painless, and I feel a victory of sorts: 2 obstacles are now crossed off my balance sheet quota, with no harm done. I ask the follow van guys if they saw the incident (they didn't) and show off my battle wound as soon as I get back in the racer van (and get no sympathy). These few drops of blood constitute the only blood drawn among the 4 of us during the entire RAAM. No one crashes into a guardrail, falls over during a rider exchange, sits on a cactus or suffers any of the other countless opportunities for injury. Aside from my TT's misfortune, we have one flat tire over the course of 3,000 miles, all due to what I want to attribute to careful preparation, the watchfulness of Greg and Taylor and, perhaps equally, a prodigious dose of good luck.

Melinda Ashley

"Part of my concern comes from what I call my husband's 'Farmer Don' syndrome, the old Yankee who would never think of stopping when it hurts or bothering to fuss with cleaning a wound, and then either forgetting or refusing to recognize it as such. It took Don many years of mountain biking tumbles and falls to accomplish the slowly but surely gradual tearing of the majority of his rotator cuff muscles in both shoulders before he'd concede to consult with an orthopedic surgeon. He preferred to chalk up the increasing pain and diminished ROM to a self- diagnosed 'arthritis', the rationale being that since there is no cure, there is no need to be pro-active about it (and take time off from biking). Six weeks after his right shoulder was surgically reconstructed in February of 2011, he was off to Spain on a cycling trip despite his doctor's alarm. Eight months later, he underwent massive surgery on the other shoulder, 8 months before the RAAM. Prior to bicycling, Don raced motorcycles and had his fair share of crashes. He truly believed that each trip to the emergency room was his first, until one day an exasperated nurse showed him his file and the many previous visits."

It's around 10 in the morning when we arrive in Switz City, IN, sunny and warming. The crew looks exhausted and upbeat at the same time, amazing people: Manny with his red headband coaxing food from the little camp stove, Lewis and Howard slapping high-fives with Dur and me, Barney showing me a text message from Melinda. All of this within the two minutes of team exchange chaos before Michael and Dave take off. I hear someone call after them, *"See you in Ohio!"* and it sinks in: We are *storming* through this section of the country. Another snooze, another state. It's quick, it's exciting, and despite the confirmation of our success, it's also getting old. I'm feeling like the cranky kid in the back of the car: *Are we there yet?* I'm so tired I forego Lydia's massage, take a quick, hot shower, eat too little too fast and fall asleep halfway into my bunk. We've been on the road for almost 100 hours since we left Oceanside and all I want is to get to the state of Maryland and its accompanying, terminal state of grace.

We wake up in Oxford, Ohio, pop. 25,000, the home of Miami University. It's a student-centered town with some nice 19th Century architecture and big shade trees, a pretty sight in the late afternoon of a pleasant day. In another hour, Michael and Dave will come in after averaging 20+ mph since Switz City. Time station # 41 in Oxford reports that our total accumulated average is 19.41 mph. Our highest accumulated average over the entire RAAM was recorded at time station # 4 in Parker AZ, at 20.24 mph when we were eager-fresh and only 286 miles from the start. Once we left Parker, our average never again reached what it is here in Oxford, OH. I sense that the crew is slightly amazed, even puzzled at our unanticipated speeds, as are we racers. *Who knew?* The crew maintains an encouraging, but professionally cautious attitude. The implicit message amongst us all is that we need to stay healthy, take no chances and hold onto our gains. We've covered 2,378 miles, and are only 615 short of Annapolis.

Even though team U4H is squeaky clean, we joke that we're insulted that no one tests us for performance enhancing drugs. At this point in the race, we're riding 3 mph faster, almost 20% faster, than the team whose record we covet. In 2004, they eclipsed a record set in 1998 by almost *2* mph. Maybe it's something extra in Manny's spaghetti, or Lydia's massages, or maybe it's because Elena Patterson has planned a celebratory banquet for Saturday evening and we don't dare be late and let her down. Whatever it is, it's working, and the strongest substances we've abused so far are Michael's triple-shot espressos, Dur's eye drops, Dave's I.V. saline infusion back in Parker, and my nap time Ambien.

As of this juncture in the 2012 RAAM, the case against Lance Armstrong hasn't yet presented all the evidence or heard the ultimate Oprah confession, but for years, the predominant belief among sophisticated cycling communities has been that Lance and most of the Tour de France riders used illegal performance enhancing drugs. The Armstrong case is additionally complicated when his cancer-support organization and inspirational yellow bracelets are taken into account. His support of cancer research is indisputable. Tens of thousands of recreational cyclists got up off the couch and adopted healthy lifestyles in no small part because Lance Armstrong brought attention to a predominantly European sport. How do these positive factors weigh against the negative? I think his unconscionable lying, bullying and deliberate intimidation of teammates and whistle-blowers tip the scales against him. The doping, at least, is a personal choice that can be made without deliberately hurting others. It appears that non-cyclists find the doping allegations much more disturbing than cyclists do. Non-cyclists want to believe that ethical athletes would refuse to use PEDs if selected to join the Tour. I'm not sure it's that simple when the realities of world championship racing include doing what everyone else does. At the top, it *is* a more or less level playing field, and it happens to involve doping.

To reach the pinnacle of bicycle racing begins by having been born genetically lucky. Your God-given VO2 max capacity must be huge and your body needs to be able to regulate the buildup of lactic acid. No amount of performance enhancing drugs can bestow these gifts upon an otherwise gifted athlete. Tour riders are universally fortunate freaks of nature. Their careers usually begin in their early teens and demand years of dedication as they move through the ranks of regional, national and international competition. So, imagine you've made cycling your life for the last decade and you're invited to join a prestigious team in the Tour de France. You're suddenly sponsored and salaried and soon-to-be famous, you're finally living the ultimate bicyclist's dream. Then comes the challenge you've not prepared for: The world-famous Tour veteran captain/God puts his arm around your shoulders and says the team doctor has something for you, the "supplements" the squad has been using all season. Your options at this point are simple: Pursue the career you've spent half your life working for, or book a coach ticket on the next plane back home to Peoria. What would you do?

The RAAM's route book directions for getting us out of Oxford confuse us in the racer van. Whether it's due to fried brains or a few street construction detours, we get lost. Daniel Boone once remarked he'd never been lost in the wilderness, but that he'd once been *mighty confused* for three days. Here in civilized Oxford, the follow van has somehow got Dur out onto the correct route, but Nate, Chris and I are possibly lost, or at least, like Daniel, we're mighty confused. We have to make a few U-turns and backtrack 3-4 blocks before we're relatively confident we're back on course. This is the first time I've been aware of missing a turn on the entire trip, and the tension is palpable. We're driving fast on hilly roads in an attempt to catch and pass the follow-van and Dur, but the farther we go without seeing them, the more we doubt ourselves. What if we're on the wrong road? Worse yet, what if we're on the right road and *Dur* is on the wrong road? Our cell phone reception is sketchy and the 2-way radios are useless. We have no way of knowing who is where. RAAM rules are explicit that under no circumstances can a racer ride backwards on the course or take a shortcut to get back on route. The only way a wrong turn can be corrected is to have the racer's crew find the racer, load him/her into a qualified RAAM team vehicle and return to the intersection where the error began. This could be especially time-consuming if the racer is off-route alone and has no cell phone, which, even if they were reliable, none of our racers carry.

It's on this leg to find and catch Dur that I become aware of how much farther 7-8 miles can seem if every moment is spent hoping to find what you want to find over the next hill or around the next bend. What makes it extra-tense is that Dur is riding very fast and we are too often impeded by card-carrying drivers of the Anti-Destination League, who seem, in Ohio, to favor impeccable Buicks of a champagne hue. After three steep hills and a lot of anxiety, we finally see and pass Dur, find a wide shoulder to pull onto and set me up for the swap. Dur comes in fast and exhausted after his 30 minute pull, too polite to chastise us for leaving him out for so long.

Nate Keck

"Thankfully, there are times when outside sources of inspiration keep us moving. One of these inspirational moments comes 40 miles east of Oxford. We'd pulled the racer van over to make a team exchange at the end of a farm's driveway. After being parked there for a few moments, I noticed the homeowner walking towards me. I headed towards him to introduce myself in hopes he wasn't upset. I was greeted with a warm smile and a brief conversation in which I described what we were doing. While I was talking with this kind gentleman, his wife and three daughters walked over to greet me as well."

It's after suppertime and I'm near the end of 7-mile pull when I spy the racer van parked in a farmer's driveway. As usual, I push extra hard into the exchange and squeeze on the brakes at the last moment. The instant I cross his wheel, Dur takes off like a rocket; we've got these trade-offs dialed into a minimum of wasted time. After Taylor straps my bike to the van, we join Nate on the lawn. He's talking to a mom and dad and their three daughters, thanking them for allowing us to stop in their driveway. They've never heard of the RAAM, but are genuinely awed by our adventure. Dad allows that he's been meaning to get an exercise bike, and now that he's met us, maybe he will. *They sell a good one at Wal-Mart.* When Nate mentions we started in California 5 days ago, Dad can't help but mention that his oldest daughter just applied to UCLA, and, with a 4.0 average, she has a good chance of being accepted. The scholar/daughter blushes profoundly and politely shushes Dad. Mom rescues her from further embarrassment by asking her to run to the house and get me a piece of cake.

Cake? I love cake, and as usual, I'm starving. Nate, Taylor and Dur have apparently already had their cake, and eaten it, too. Miss UCLA is back in a minute with a huge slice of angel food cake topped with strawberries and whipped cream. *Damn!* It is arguably the best cake I have ever tasted, ever. Thirty seconds later, it's all gone, the fork is licked clean and Nate says it's time to go. We're lavish with our thanks and wish the daughter early acceptance at UCLA. Before we drive off, Mom reminds us to be safe, and adds, *"We'll pray for you."*

Five minutes down the road, we pass Dur, wave and shout, and speed on to the next exchange. Just before I leave the van, I notice he's left his piece of cake, half-eaten, on the top of the cooler beside me. The discipline required to train for the RAAM is nothing compared to what it takes for me to leave Dur's cake uneaten. But. I. Do. A few minutes later, after we've made our exchange and I'm flying high on performance-enhancing, white sugar dope and heartfelt, heartland prayers. I'll always think of this section in Ohio as the sweetest 7 miles of my race across America.

The fatigue leads to goofiness at the rider exchanges. We all seem to be imploding into ourselves, still doing what we have to do but ridding ourselves of social barriers, too tired to be anyone other than who we are, or perhaps, exactly who we were at age 12. During one waiting session for Dur, Nate finds a hand-painted, cardboard sign alongside the road with the words, GUN SHOW hand-painted in black. With his biceps bulging out from under the short sleeves of his RAAM T-shirt, Nate poses for on-coming traffic with the sign in one hand and his "guns" flexed. Cars honk and Taylor takes pictures. At another stop, I dangle a discarded cigarette butt nonchalantly from my lip while Nate points the camera. He sends it to my coach, Tom Scotto, with the caption, *"Training hard as usual."* None of this is remotely ingenious, but of course we think it's hysterical.

For the next fifty miles or so, Dur and I go from elevations of 600 ft. up to almost 1,200 at Highland and Leesburg -- I think. I've become accustomed to not knowing where I am in Ohio, much of which we ride in the dark. Night riding was feathery fast and exciting at the beginning of the RAAM. Now, the soaring bird has become the boring bullock, and a netting of mental and physical fatigue is being drawn tighter at every rotation. When I try to do the ritual bike and body inventory I began in Oceanside -- legs, feet, shoulders, chamois, neck, toes, tires, chain, derailleurs, brakes, helmet . . . . *what else*? It gets all mixed up. I feel I have to start back at the beginning because the order makes no sense and I don't want miss something that requires attention. RAAMbrain has hijacked my attention span and I'm too tired to get much of it back. I paraphrase Mose Allison and start singing *My mind is on vacation, but my legs are working overtime.* I try not to worry about the legs, which isn't easy; they hurt. My knee hurts. There are times, however, in this 5th day of the RAAM, when it feels as if I'm in an alternative reality, detached from that familiar pair of legs, watching from high above as they rise and fall on auto pilot, pedaling, pedaling. Mose Allison's refrain is echoed with a convoluted dip into cut-rate philosophy as I tailor Descartes', *"I think, therefore I am"* to the more fitting RAAM refrain: *"I pedal, therefore I am."* I'm still coherent enough, to recognize that, *"I think, therefore I pedal,"* would be oxymoronic.

Ohio is supposed to be the last easy state. I'd hoped it was going to be the interlude in which we pulled together all our energies before for the final push, but it feels as if the final lap gun has gone off early. Ohio is a pretty state, but so were Indiana, Illinois and Missouri. I keep seeing roadside signs pointing to tiny Midwest towns with modest names this New England native never heard of -- Thrifton, Lattaville, Vigo -- and I wonder if we're trapped in the cyclists' version of the movie, *Groundhog Day.* This

158

recurrent sense of *déjà vu*, the monotony of repetitive exchanges and the 20-minute, go-stop-go routine is becoming as mentally tedious as it is physically. The day before we left California, we racers were consumed with nervous energy in anticipation of the week to come. We were instructed to rest and relax while the crew attended to hundreds of last-minute details. All *we* wanted was to be on the road in rollicking, raging, race mode. At lunch that day, Michael and I used an identical term to express our itchiness to start the race: *"Let's do this thing,"* we said, almost simultaneously. *Let's get on with it.* Now, I'm beginning to think more along the lines of, *"We've done this thing. Let's get on with getting this thing over with."* I'm plenty tired, but perhaps even worse, I'm bored.

As the boredom becomes more palpable, *pedal, pedal,* it gets me thinking about, *pedal, pedal,* what would add some spice and variation, *pedal, pedal,* to this thing that has become so pedaling boring. When Dave was sidelined back in California, the challenge of continuing on with just 3 of us re-energized my appreciation for adventure. I don't want to repeat that painful event, and I don't want us to fall short of our goal, but an unexpected crisis requiring an ingenious solution would provide a welcome interlude to this tedious routine. Of course, none of us would *cause* the interlude. It would arrive as a *"Deus ex machina,"* the ancient Greek theatrical device by which a God's intervention frees the characters from responsibility. *Not my fault!* Even if it costs us a few minutes, some odd encounter might improve our mental outlook enough to actually make us go faster. So, I'm thinking it would be nice if, say, a bridge washed out and we had to make a raft or swim our bikes across a river -- in the dark. How exciting would *that* be compared with what we're doing? This endless pedaling tedium would definitely disappear if we had to ride through a herd of feral hogs. *Oink, oink!* Three or four minutes of *that* would compete with any adventure we've had so far. And it wouldn't take long to stop and put out a school bus fire, save the kiddies and ride off in a 2-wheeled imitation of the Lone Ranger, *would it?*

Dur and I swap endless 20-minute shifts and pedal into the RAAM's Day Five tedium as if we were two Sisyphusian hamsters spinning in a cage. Somewhere near McArthur, an illuminated roadside sign for a community college grabs my attention and I decide to do some mental exercises instead of wishing for a fantastical, porcine intervention. A math problem will do. Pedal, pedal, pedal; how many pedal strokes in the Race Across America? Should be easy, but I need to make some simple assumptions since I'm doing it in my head. For simplicity's sake, I'll assume the race takes 6 days and the rider's cadence averages 80 rpm. My cadence is typically higher, but there are stops and steep climbs and the math will be easier with an even number. So, 24 hours, times 60 minutes, times 6 days, times 80 rpm is the problem I need to solve -- not making a raft to cross a river. I round up the 24 to make it easier, call it 25 hours times 60 minutes, which is easy -- 1,500. I repeat 1,500 a few times to burn it into my frazzled brain --1,500, 1,500 -- which, multiplied by 6 days is still easy -- 9,000. And now, the 9,000 multiplied by 80 rpm is also easy, 720,000. I think. . . But since we'll be more than 6 days and I underestimated cadence rpm, I round it up to 900,000. 900,000 pedal strokes to ride across the country. Sounds exhausting, but then I have to remember each member of the team can claim only one quarter, 225,000. Still sounds impressive. I can't wait to finish my shift and get in the van and tell the guys how many pedal strokes it takes to ride across the country, but when I start to explain how I did the math in my head, I fall victim to RAAMbrain and decide to eat a sandwich instead.

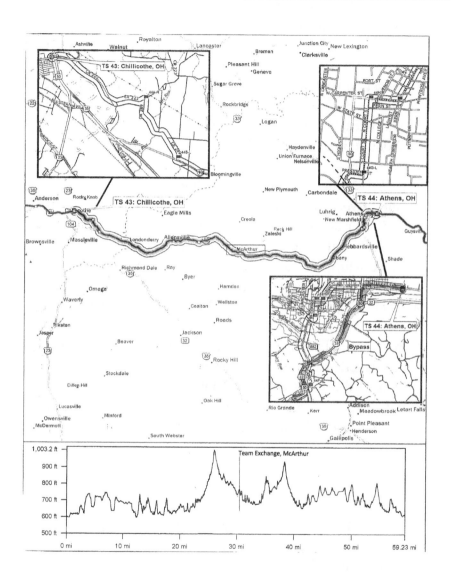

It's 1:30 in the morning when we finally finish the hilly 140 miles from Oxford to the team exchange in McArthur, Ohio, where we are just 45 miles short of the West Virginia line. This will have been one of the shorter rotations of the RAAM, but we have ridden all but 55 miles across a state with endless rollies, and still averaged over 19 mph. The elevation back at the Mississippi River in Alton, Ill. was 400 ft. above sea level. We were up to 1,200 ft. in Highland and Leesburg, OH, but 150 miles east of here, we'll see 3,000 ft. in Gormania, WV.

From here in McArthur, there are 478 miles remaining, and we're told it will be broken into three shifts: Michael and Dave will ride 161 miles from McArthur to Grafton, WV, Dur and I will ride 160 miles from Grafton to Cove Gap, 20 miles east of Hancock, MD, where Michael and Dave will begin the final, 157-mile, downhill-ish ride to the finish. This means that Dur and I have just completed our next-to last leg of the RAAM. What this adventure has taught me so far is that my body is capable of pushing past limits I thought were unattainable, while my mind has resorted to survival strategies of a nature I'd never imagined within me. Now, all that remains is to make sure this combination works over the RAAM's most difficult challenge, the Appalachian Mountains.

"One trouble with growing older is that it gets progressively tougher to find a famous historical figure who didn't amount to much when he was your age."

Bill Vaughn

DAY SIX
McArthur, OH to Annapolis, Md.
478 miles

It's 10 a.m. on June 22nd in Grafton, WV. Dur and I are feeling better after 4 hours of sleep despite the RVs awkward progress across narrow, 2-lane roads. We can hardly complain about the RV's lack of comfort: The 161 miles that Michael and Dave rode from McArthur while we rested included dozens of grueling 200 to 400-ft. hills through eastern Ohio and western West Virginia. Despite the climbing, their average speed between McArthur and time station # 46 here in Grafton is well over 18 mph. We also learn that our average accumulated speed across the country is now 19.34 mph.

Grafton, pop 5,100, lies in a valley at a little over 1,100 ft. elevation. Like so many of the Blue Highway towns we've passed through east of the Mississippi, Grafton is yet another in the grips of slow decline. Too much of the modestly handsome 1800s architecture suffers from disrepair, too many fields lay fallow and too many storefronts are vacant. The end of viable agriculture, loss of traffic to the nearby Interstate and the lack of industry have unfortunately left these little jewels of Americana behind, but as a picture postcard journey of what this country looked like 100 years ago, there are few routes more authentic than this.

The sun is shining and the sky is blue when Dur and I begin this 162-mile pull out of Grafton, which the RAAM route book describes as: *"A treacherous two lane road with long steep climbs. Some precipitous drops if you go over a guard rail."* After the first 12 miles, we begin a 5-mile climb on a 6% grade up to 2,500 ft. followed by a quick, 3-mile plunge down to 1,400 ft. We catch our breaths on 4 miles of fast, level terrain, then start the grind again to 2,500 ft. at mile 30. If only the climbs were as easy as the countryside is beautiful! A roadside sign indicates we're inside the southwest tip of Maryland at around mile 35, and then 5 miles later, another sign declares we're back in WV when we cross over the North Branch of the Potomac in the 3,000-ft. high settlement of Gormania. The blue skies we saw a few hours ago are fringed with gray, and the temperature is dropping into the comfortable 70s, but the very suggestion of rain has been so absent from our RAAM so far that I ignore the evidence gathering on the western horizon. We push across another 20 miles and another bunch of 200-ft. peaks to mile 60 and a long-awaited, 5-mile descent down a 9% grade into Keyser, WV. The hill is twisty and beautifully paved, delicious road candy. The altitude is but a fraction of what it was in Arizona and Colorado, but the downhill plunge is reminiscent of the descent through Jerome to Cottonwood, and it is again my good fortune to be its navigator, a responsibility I dispatch with all the speed and energy I can muster.

The Appalachians have more elevation gain per horizontal mile than any portion of the race. The Rocky mountains were dramatic and much higher, but the grades, although longer, were less steep. The Rockies offered huge, distant views, a big sky and a sense of wide open spaces, while here in the east, the lush vegetation looms up and over the narrow roads in a protective closeness. Riding these old mountains require a mindset that accommodates repetitive insult. The legs must ignore in-coming evidence of self-destruction and the brain must be disregarded as if it were a noisy saboteur. If finding one's limits requires pushing beyond one's limits, welcome to Maryland -- state

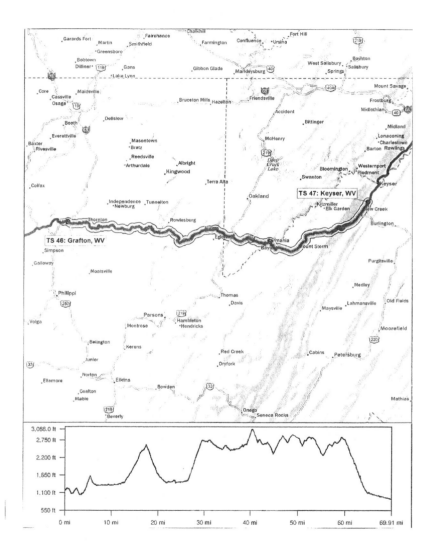

flower, the black-eyed Susan. If the purpose of racing the RAAM is to discover a deeper understanding of oneself -- or to be rid of the self you'd rather be rid of, welcome to Maryland, birthplace of Eubie Blake, Babe Ruth and one of our un-likeliest of Vice-Presidents, Spiro Agnew. Welcome, cyclist, to The Old Line State.

With 5-1/2 days of RAAMracing under my chamois, I'm dog-tired but still tend to favor optimism over the incoming evidence. Although it's never been discussed, part of our team's unspoken culture discourages talk about infirmity. Since our average speed puts us well above our goal, each of my teammates and I want to believe the other 3 must be in good health, and like religion, this belief is based on desperate faith rather than factual evidence. I have no idea how Michael and Dave are *really* faring, but I assign to them qualities with which I'm familiar. If it takes a village to raise a record-breaking team, we are the 4 lucky beneficiaries of the generous villagers on the crew and our loved ones back home. I envision Michael, the Sultan of Cycling, reigning the roads with quiet composure and dignity. I see Daredevil Dave, our Energizer Bunny, as the unstoppable master of the mountains. And I know that the Dur of end<u>ur</u>ance, the *Dur* of <u>dur</u>ability, never falters, never fails. And me? I occasionally feel fast, furious and scrappy, then tedious and crappy, and too seldom quicker in wit than in groundspeed.

I'm most familiar by far with Dur's ride, but his dauntless demeanor may mask all sorts of complaints. *"How's it going, Dur?"* is invariably answered with an ambiguous grunt and a shrug, which in RAAMspeak, means, *The question is irrelevant. What good would it do to complain?* I play the same game. *"Feeling good!"* means I will see this through to Annapolis. We're all about Soviet-style stoicism -- *stubborn macho mules* would not be an unfair definition -- but how else to survive an experience which offers no remedy to whining? If there were something we could *do* to ease one another's pain, I'm sure we would, but of course, there is nothing to be done but proclaim, *"Feeling good!"* and keep on riding. This is exactly what baffles and troubles my wife about the endurance sports' culture, and, absent an intelligent rebuttal, which I've so far been unable to formulate, I can only sympathize with her point of view.

I'm free to confess to *myself* that three toes on my right foot are permanently numb, my neck aches like hell from terminal TT torture, and my left knee feels as it has a needle stuck in it when I stand to pedal. I'm perpetually drowning in gallons of electrolyte mix to forestall the constant threat of cramping, and I would seriously consider selling my dear grandmother into slavery in exchange for Lance Armstrong's performance enhancers. Until Ohio, I was able to take off at sprint speed as soon as Dur's wheel crossed mine. My heart, lungs and legs were amenable to these sudden starts and I could reach a sustainable pace quickly. Pre-RAAM, our team's recurring concern was that a 20-minute segment would be too short; we worried we'd have no time to warm up, but once the RAAM began, we realized our worries were unfounded, and they were -- until now. In these last, nasty miles, I begin to experience vasospasms in my legs at the start of every pull. My exhausted femoral arteries, relaxed and contracted during the 20 minutes' rest in the van, are increasingly slow to dilate when my sudden-sprint start calls for more blood. The result is severe aching in the quads and abductors and a hint of feeling faint. It lasts less than a minute, but it hurts -- a lot -- so I ought to be timid off the line. But I wouldn't be doing this if I were timid, so I push even harder, ignoring the brain and digging deeper into the pain. The best I can do is to try and compartmentalize the vasospasms. They are illegally invading my body. but they are not *me*. While the shopworn phrase, "No pain, no gain" is popular among body builders and football players, the endurance junkie's version has to be, in this case, "No pain, no brain."

We ride north along the West Virginia side of the border with Maryland, close to the North Branch of the Potomac between Keyser, WV, and Cumberland, MD. There are two, 400-ft. climbs and three other shorter humps over this 28-mile section, but they seem surprisingly manageable. The storm clouds that have dogged us all afternoon finally deliver a light but inconsequential rain in Cumberland. The road surface gets slippery during the hour it takes the rain to pass. I'm self-consciously cautious about crashing on the downhill sections, but there are no panicked moments, and aside from road dirt on our bikes and legs, the rain is a welcome diversion. From time station #48 in Cumberland, the finish is figuratively within sight (217 miles), but the notorious 37-mile stretch between Cumberland and Hancock is about to begin.

From the RAAM route book
"The four major climbs in this section are tough. The last climb (up Sideling Hill) could be a walker. In Hancock, the route is 2 blocks from the Potomac River. The river has dropped 1,900 feet since we crossed the North Branch in Gormania!"

Somewhere in this nastiest of nasty sections, I've just begun my shift and am struggling up yet another 900-ft. rise at a crippled snail's pace, resigned to discomfort until my reunion with Dur and the crew at the top of the mountain. *Don't think, keep moving.* White Oak and gum trees arch over the narrow road which is bordered by a lush tangle of ferns and rhododendron. This road has little traffic, few crossroads, no houses and a peacefully quiet environment, odd juxtapositions for experiencing the many fulsome flavors of fatigue. *Every mile left behind is one less ahead,* I keep reminding myself.

In the distance, ahead, I hear a high-pitched, screechy sound and imagine an exotic bird whose call is unknown to my New England-tuned ears. As I draw nearer, the intervals between the screeches decrease and I picture a frenzied, avian courtship being consummated, wings beating, feathers ruffled, Nature fulfilled. Pedaling closer still, my addled RAAMbrain improbably imagines this shriek-screech racket to be an avant-garde version of the theme from *Deliverance*, played on a gap-toothed, mountain man's, ill-gotten boom box. I feebly laugh at myself for toying with this absurd idea, then laugh out loud when I realize I'm grateful that the follow van is close behind to protect me from dangers both real and imagined. But-- do they hear what I hear? Do they hear me *laughing?* Here in the woods of WV, I'm wondering if this is what it feels like to be finally losing my marbles.

As I pull even with this mountainside clamor, I search the shady undergrowth for the source of the sound, which is now reduced to jagged squeaks and grunts. *What the hell?* I instinctively slow my pedaling when I see the tops of bushes jerk and sway across the ditch a few yards away from me. *Should I get off and wait to see what's going on here?* Does racing the RAAM prohibit random, roadside curiosity? *Of course it doesn't, you fool. Keep pedaling!* The bushes shudder again, and this time, the movement is accompanied by whimpers and gasps. Goosebumps dot my forearms and I pedal faster. *Jesus!* Looking back over my shoulder, I see an opening in the dense vegetation and the bloody hind legs of a rabbit being dragged away into the forest.

Inevitably, I catch sight of the van up ahead, and Dur, with Nate and Taylor beside him. The affection I've developed for Dur over these five days is embodied in this image of him waiting for me at these rider swaps, Dur a-straddle his bike, one foot poised on the pedal, one foot on the road, head and shoulders turned to gauge my arrival. The hill is so steep it takes me another 4-5 minutes to reach him, but as usual, the closer I get, the faster I go and the moment I am off the bike I feel better -- or, certainly, less awful. Nate straps my bike to the van rack, I climb in the back seat and rummage through the cooler for a few-hundred calories of food and drink. I've never stopped being hungry since we left Oceanside. The metabolic engine driving me is an unrepentant, voracious *fuel-hog*.

Nate Keck and Dr. Brent Ruby from the Montana Center for Work Physiology and Exercise Metabolism (The University of Montana) conducted a detailed energy expenditure evaluation on our team over the course of the 2012 RAAM. Their experiment measured weight gain/loss and calorie consumption from Oceanside to Annapolis.

Nate Keck

"Prior to publication in a sports-science journal, the specific details are currently privileged, but the gist of the findings show that septuagenarians such as the T430 racers are capable of roughly twice the amount of energy expenditure as previously reported in active, age-matched men. What impacts the number of Calories burned has as much to do with body size than anything. For example, a bigger person is going to burn more Calories than a small person just to stay functioning and supply the additional body mass with sufficient energy supplies. To arrive at meaningful conclusions, the

Caloric content of the food ingested has to be measured, which this experiment did not allow, but on average, the T430 racers burned approximately 60,000-70,000 Calories over the course of our 6.55 day performance. Their average daily energy expenditures were similar to "easier" days' performances in the Tour de France. With few exceptions, the T430 racers were able to match the energy demands of the ride with their food/fuel intake. With slight shifts in body weight recorded at intervals during the race, the following data show weights recorded the night before the event began and at the finish line ceremonies in Annapolis: Michael's weight dropped from 170 to 169 lbs, Dur's from 159 to 153 lbs, Don's from 160 to 154 lbs and Dave's from 143 to 140 lbs. "

Race-day cyclists are supposed to stay off their feet as much as possible. Some coaches even discourage recreational walking; you're either on the bike or sitting/ lying down. Nate is working on an M.S. in exercise science, but he apparently hasn't sipped that particular brand of No-Stand Kool-Aid, or maybe he figures it doesn't pertain to RAAM elders on the cusp of victory. In any case, I'm not inclined to sit inside a hot van doing nothing on a sunny Appalachian afternoon, so here we three are, 6 miles up the road, standing around the back of the van stretching our legs and trading small talk while we wait for Dur. In a variation of our custom since Kansas, Taylor picks up a stone and wings it at the galvanized guard rail on the opposite side of the road. *Whaang!* Perfect shot! Before the echo fades, Nate and I are gathering up our own mini-arsenals, and for the next 10 minutes, we pock that innocent guardrail with volleys of pebbles and rocks. Overhand, underhand, sidearm, behind-the-back, jump shot -- our choreography is at once artful, awful, self-deprecating and therapeutically perfect. Each hit is followed with cheers, each miss followed by, *almost!* This diversion from crushing fatigue is as goofy as it is restorative. It feels great to be 12-years old again for 10 minutes. With Dur in sight, Nate digs loose a rock the size of a butterball turkey and muscles it across the road. Whooping triumphantly, he humps it up over the guardrail. We trade congratulatory high fives as it hops, bumps and crashes through boulders and brush, hurtling into the deep gulley below. *Yesss!!* The final crash-thump signals the juggernaut has come to its rest just before Dur pulls into sight, looking strong and resolute. I watch him pick up speed over the last, steep 100 yards and I think, *how the hell does he do it?*

Earline Higgins

"Training for RAAM brought some changes to our routines which were already heavily centered around Dur's bike racing. Since Dur's coach had scheduled many days of riding 5-6 hours' ride inside, my family room became a gym with the bicycle-on-trainer set up in front of our big TV. There he was, equidistant from the TV, kitchen and bathroom, and right under the ceiling fan. All not so bad except that his trainer was extremely noisy from the extreme wear from overuse (he got a new, much quieter one AFTER the RAAM). He would dread these long workouts such that he put them off until too late in the day where it interfered with my preparation and serving of our evening meal. I finally had to threaten that if he was not done by 5pm, I was not serving dinner! The threat worked -- most of the time.

To follow Team U4H progress during the race I kept track via the U4H website blog, Barney's blog and the RAAM website which allowed me to follow him on my own course map with time stations marked. I would always know where Dur was and whether he was on or off shift. I would even get up during the night to check to see if they made it to the time stations on schedule. This was my only way of keeping up with him, since he did not call me until the 4th day! And he might not have called then except I had sent him a message, via one of the crewmembers, to call me. And he finally did -- the next day. We have always said he has a one track mind, and it was all for the RAAM during the RAAM.

After reading how well they were doing, by Sunday morning I realized I might have to alter my travel plans to arrive in Annapolis on time for their finish. As early as Sunday evening, I was so confident in our guys beating the target arrival time, that I called and moved my motel reservations and departure up by one day. I drove up from Chattanooga to Annapolis alone, a 2-day trip of 625 miles.

Another thing that I concentrated on was Dur's nutritional intake. With the excessive training, his coach, Aidan Charles, advised him to add more protein, calcium, etc. Our daughter, who is a Registered Dietician also aided me in this area. She became so intrigued with the RAAM that she had the whole Dialysis Clinic where she works watching the websites and following the race. By the end of the week she was also getting up during the night to check the progress. I would call all our five children every day to keep them updated. All our many Facebook friends and family were forwarded RAAM-tracking websites, and it was amazing, the numbers of them who reported they followed the team's progress with so much interest -- even high school classmates from 50 years ago."

Dur's wheel crosses mine and I take off, vasospasms raging. It feels brutally awful, but our brief spell of mindless fun chucking rocks renews my strength and I ignore the pain as best I can. Soon enough, the hill levels off and I'm back in the zone. Another few minutes, and I'm on a blessedly fast downhill grade, reeling in fast, easy miles. I relax into to a wave of exhausted gratitude for Nate and Taylor and Dur and Michael and Dave and Barney and *all* our stalwart crew making this crazy adventure possible. With the downhill speed picking up, I'm deliriously high, still smiling at the image of Nate letting the boulder loose over the guardrail. From the dismal depression of uphill efforts to the manic exhilaration of gravity-assisted free fall, I'm a bi-polar poster boy, flying along as if this were the embodiment of ecstasy on wheels. I believe that we *will* in fact keep it together all the way to Annapolis, that this ride *is going* to be the once-in-a-lifetime, kickass thrill I hoped it would be. *Woo-hah!* to the eastbound army of Team T430. Genuflections to Our Lady of Perpetual Pedaling! I'm thinking, *yup, yup, yup, this is it!* and I keep pushing faster and faster.

It comes up much too suddenly: A tunnel of deep shade over the roadbed obscures a deep, crusty cavity in the pavement. I'm on a sharp, downhill curve and riding too fast to miss it. I center-punch the hole, bounce up out of it and am airborne with my front wheel pointed in a perilous direction. This all takes only a nanosecond, and how I respond comes strictly from muscle memory; the *thinking* cortex is much too slow to process and instruct on such short notice. In order to get my wheels straightened out, I pedal hard, a reflex so counter-intuitive that it takes many repetitions to absorb. *"Momentum is your friend"* is a staple of mountain-biking lore, and it's also an apt, if obvious, metaphor for dealing with life's tough patches, as in, *"Keep trying. Tackle the problem square on, don't give up."* It's an unseemly directive while waiting mid-air for the wheels to make an uncertain contact with the road, but with luck, it's a consistently proven solution. And now, it works again. Three or four intense pedal strokes pull me back into my line of travel.

This is the fourth time on the RAAM I've been too close to crashing; the previous 3 were due to sudden winds gusts at high speeds on the TT and the subsequent speed wobble, not my doing: Kansas and Durango come to mind. I had no control over the wind, but this time I am stupidly at fault, so giddy with optimism, courting that reckless edge where irreversible things happen. I slow down and resettle my priorities, remember my promise to Melinda. The rabbit's bloody legs invade my thoughts and I realize that the only predator threatening me is the monster of vain ambition.

Melinda Ashley

"If I have to think about it -- and how can I not? -- the thought that Don might die trying to win is less horrific than the thought that he might be maimed.

All of us at some level have fears of a loved-one becoming paralyzed, but in most of our circles of family and friends, it does not become a reality. In our family, this has not been the case. Within the past 6 years, we have had 2 healthy, vibrant and exuberant men become quadriplegics. Both died from complications in the past year and a half. Tom Luckey, a college friend of Don's, fell out a window and broke his neck. My brother Robin contracted ALS (Lou Gehrig's disease). Both men went through years of intense suffering, required immense amounts of care resulting in huge impacts on their families. The care required for my brother Rob after he could no longer eat or speak was beyond imaginable. One of the things my family was grateful for was that a few years prior to becoming ill, Robin (also a risk taker, an avid skier and mountaineer in extreme conditions) accepted that something serious could happen to him and took out a long-term care health insurance policy, which saved his family from the financial ruin healthcare costs can impose on a serious disability. So, experiencing the far-reaching aspects of a disabled family member is extremely fresh and real for me. If Don were to die racing his bicycle, he insists he couldn't think of a better way to go -- 'if' being the operative word here. But to imagine what would happen if he were to lose the use of his body was something I struggled with every day of the race."

John, Ken and Greg in the follow-van have the most unique view of this race. Except for a few congested sections such as in Sedona, AZ, and West Alton, MO, they've witnessed every pedal stroke turned by the four racers. They've watched us creep up and fly down the steepest inclines, they've seen us blown across the roads in Kansas and held their breaths as we cleverly threaded through traffic in towns and cities all across the country. At speeds beyond 15 mph, there's usually enough wind turbulence in the racers' ears to cancel out the sound of the follow-van, but on the steep hills in WV and MD, I can hear its motor changing revs as the automatic transmission labors to find lower and lower ratios. Once again I'm grateful to these guys for their protection and reassurances, but for the first time, I'm self-conscious about my performance being observed, which may be a vain presumption on my part, but it haunts me nonetheless. Each of us racers has probably wondered at some point if we were the fastest or slowest of the four, and each of us has probably wondered how our weariest moments were being evaluated by the 2 sets of eyes in the follow van. Early on in the race, follow van driver/navigator John Markley mentioned he could tell when I was getting tired because my knees would get wider apart, a definite no-no in biking bio-mechanics. Ever since his remark, I've been conscious of keeping my knees together, and my legs, from hip to ankle in a single plane. Aside from John's (helpful) observation, I'm convinced that the constant encouraging remarks and psychological support from all three of these patient guys add an intangible bit of energy to every pedal stroke.

Sideling Hill, the last dreadful climb before Hancock, is as brutish as advertised. I pedal my lowest gear at the highest cadence bearable, as if the gyroscopic effect alone will keep me going. It's on this hill that Team 26 racer, Lasse Ibert, came upon Daniel Telep (of the PAC Masters 80+ team), walking his bike up the hill. In a show of true sportsmanship, Ibert dismounted and walked the last 100 yards of the hill in solidarity with the 78 yr-old Telep before speeding onward to win the 4-person division. Telep is exactly 3 times Ibert's age, and while neither was the youngest or oldest in the race, the three generations between them demonstrate the RAAM's appeal to all ages.

On the 37 miles from Hell to Hancock, Dur and I are on cusp of exhaustion. I know the signs well enough to tell he is as trashed as I am, and we still have some gnarly miles left in our shift, although exactly how many, we don't know. Six months before the race, Dave Eldridge mapped out our team exchanges based on his encyclopedic knowledge of the route. At our training session in Tucson, he handed out 9 pages of mileages and elevation profiles between each of the 18 team exchange points across the country. Assumptions were made about which 2-man team

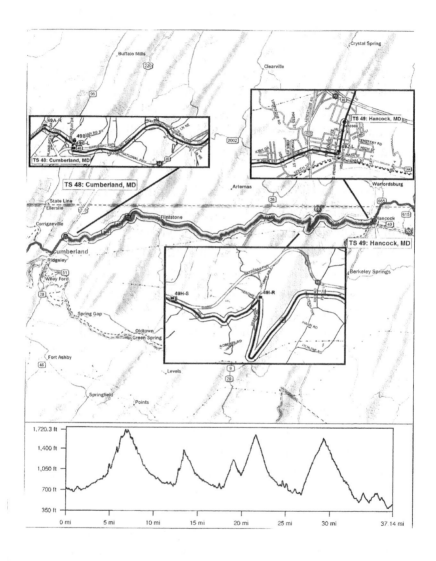

would ride when and where, and we dutifully scribbled it down. With that information in hand, we racers could *theoretically* anticipate exactly when we would be on the road, what to expect in terms of terrain and mileage, and how to pace ourselves accordingly.

The reality of the road, however, means that we racers quickly lose Dave's pages in the chaos of musical chairs at team exchanges, and we leave our schedules entirely up to the racer van crew. The only time I see mileages and terrain profiles is when I get a quick glimpse at the crew's route book on the dashboard. Those 20-minute shifts in the van require too much attention to rest, nutrition, hydration and ice packs to allow for any kind of coherent attention to maps and numbers. Until now, I rarely ask about the length or nature of my next pull; no matter how tired, I could always find the energy to ride what needed to be ridden. I might ask for an *estimate* to the team exchange, but in these final miles of the Appalachians, my dependency upon the crew -- *exactly* how much farther do we have to go, *precisely* -- has become as unflatteringly obsessive for me as it must be maddeningly tedious to them.

When Dur commented about Nate's under-reporting distances between Flagstaff and Tuba City, I didn't understand why he found it so vexing, but now I do. Until now, when I heard X number of miles were left to the next team exchange, I'd think of X as a workable distance for *me -- alone --* without bothering to parse it into halves and splitting it with Dur. Now, not only do I divide by 2, but I find myself calculating the likelihood of my having 3 more pulls compared with 2 for Dur, or vice versa. This sudden, selfish concern for every mile ahead is aggravated by my paranoia that the crew is deliberately under-reporting. At the beginning of my last shift, I apologized for asking yet again, *how many more miles?*

But when they respond to the same annoying question before my *next* shift, the math doesn't make sense. Forty minutes ago, they said we have 30 miles left. I rode for 20 minutes and Dur rode for 20 minutes. Even at a crawl, we had to have ridden 10 miles combined, but now, I'm about to go out again and am told we have "only" 25 miles left. I understand their strategy, and I might try the same thing if I were coaxing a pack of old dogs over the mountains. I can't be angry with them, after all they've sacrificed for us; I only want it to be over.

East of Rouzerville, PA, we cross the Appalachian Trail, the longest continuously marked footpath in the world. Covering 2,180 miles, it traverses 14 states between Springer Mt, GA, and Maine's Mt. Katahdin. Nearby Harper's Ferry, VA, marks the A.T.'s midpoint. I have a special affection for the A.T., especially where it weaves through my hometown of Lyme, NH. For many years I maintained a portion of the trail between Reservoir Pond Rd. and the top of Smarts Mountain. The flights of stone steps I built up to and along Lambert Ridge remain in place today, sturdy emblems of fond, summer memories.

And suddenly, it's over. Near the top of an 800-ft climb, we make our final team exchange at around 8 o'clock in the evening. It's difficult to absorb the finality of the moment, but it's here: Dur and I have completed our part of the RAAM. *There is no more for us to do.* I'm struck with the paradoxical emotion of being relieved it's over and the desire to continue. Watching Michael and Dave depart for the final 157 miles is bitter sweet in a way I would never have predicted. *Wait! I want to go with you!* We've come so far through so much with such constancy that I finally dare believe we've become a true team and accomplished a rare and preposterous thing.

Michael and Dave are riding the last shift of the race when the route passes near the Gettysburg battlefields. One of my mother's ancestors was George Brooke Garnett, 1817-1863. A West Point graduate and Brigadier General in the Confederate Army, he had the poor judgment to lead himself and his men to slaughter in the notoriously ill-planned Pickett's charge. Dur and I are asleep in a moving vehicle a few miles south of the hill where he was shot dead from his horse on July 3rd, 1863 -- 149 years and 19 days ago. The temperature was reported to be 87 degrees, identical to ours this afternoon. Garnett's only progeny, Billy Garnett, was 8 years-old when his father died at the age of 46. My kids are 44 and 46, my granddaughters are both 6. I'm 72 this year, 2012. Billy Garnett's Oglala Lakota mother, named Looking Woman, was 15 when Billy was born. The General never married her or acknowledged his half-breed son. Billy Garnett died in 1930 at 75, in Wyoming, having served as interpreter between the Sioux and the U.S. Army before, during and long after, the battle of Little Big Horn. We are 150 miles from the end of a 3,000-mile march, done in the name of adventure. General Garnett was 50 yards from the Union Army's entrenched position behind a stone wall on Cemetery Ridge when his march ended, done in the name of Secession. We sleep in the comfort of conditioned air in a recreational vehicle. I imagine my ancestor's last moments were shrouded in the smoke and roar and screaming chaos of battle. If all goes well with Michael and Dave, our 19-person army will arrive intact and safe in Annapolis in about 8 hours. One hundred and forty-nine years ago, 500 men under my ancestor's command lost their lives in 60 minutes' time. A few hours after our arrival in Annapolis, we'll eat blueberry-pancakes and bacon for breakfast before slipping between 400-count cotton sheets at a swell hotel, embraced in love and the satisfied slumber of Victory.

Ken Gunnells

"On the last night, not far from the end, I'm trying to tell Dave he is about to cross the finish line, and he still doesn't understand me. I am so fatigued and so sick of our lack of communication that I tell him -- over the PA system -- to put it where the sun doesn't shine. At the dock, Dave sticks out his hand to thank me. I almost refuse, but the race is over, we had a great success, and it occurs to me that the PA system was lousy and that Dave is probably just plain deaf.

After the awards ceremony at the dock in Annapolis, I find the pebble I've carried east from the Pacific. As the sun comes up, I take a picture of it, thank God for a safe journey and toss it in the Atlantic."

Dave Burnett

"Don and Dur were out on the road slugging away at the toughest section of our entire ride, the nasty hills, twisty roads and poor pavement of West Virginia and a small arm of Maryland that reaches into West Virginia. There was some uncertainty as to just when they would finish their last pull when Michael and I would take over till the end. I recall being surprised at how long Dave Eldridge was leaving them out on the road. I had made it known to Dave that I was ready and eager to get going. But he had great faith in Don and Dur. They stayed out and completed almost all the nasty hills and then we finally got our shot at the final leg of our journey.

I soon realized that despite all my enthusiasm and willingness to get going, the reality was that I was tired and slow. It seemed impossible to get my bike flying. We had taken over around dusk and Michael and I proceeded into the night, but even getting to 17 mph on the flats seemed like an impossible task. I treasured my break times in the racer van; they were over all too soon. I even began to suspect that the crew was using me more than my legitimate percentage of the time. Was a bit of paranoia was creeping in? But on and on, into the night we did slog.

As we worked through the hills, I became aware that we were precariously close to losing our 19 + mph overall average. We knew that we had the overall record, but staying above 19 mph now supplanted the original goal, and I was determined to save that symbolic, 19-plus average. So, struggle we did. I remember Michael urging me on at one point as I took over. 'GO, GO, GO, Dave!' I tried, but it still didn't happen. I was so slow, and yet it felt like it was up to Michael and me to maintain that average or else we would be letting the team down.

And then a magical thing happened at 10 miles from the end of the RAAM. I was in the racer van and we passed the first woman solo rider, Trix Zgraggen, from Switzerland. She had started RAAM 4 days before us and there she was. Somehow in my fatigued fog, she looked beautiful. We stopped the racer van with 7 miles to go and waited by the side of the road for Michael. As the crew was discussing whether to let me go to the end, or break it up with 3 miles to go and put Michael back out, she rode by us. I said to the crew, 'Let me have the whole distance. I'll fly!' They said okay, and soon Michael arrived. With words of encouragement, off I went. Oh my god, that beautiful woman made me a different rider. Suddenly I had legs. I looked down at my speedometer under street lights and saw 23 MPH on the flats. I could never have imagined such a transformation. It felt like the first day, exhilarating. And soon, there she was. I was going 2 feet for every 1 of hers. I overtook her so fast that despite my desire to talk with her, our conversation was limited to my brief, "hello" and her asking me if I was a solo rider. I tried to respond, but I doubt she could have heard me. My strong legs lasted to the finish and we saved our 19+ mph average, 19.04 to be exact.

There is one more recollection. The entire way across the country the follow van had communicated with the riders through a small, inadequate speaker mounted to the van's roof. To add to this squawky speaker problem, one of the follow car drivers was from the Deep South. I had serious problems understanding him. With one half mile to go he said, 'Half a mile left.' I heard, 'left,' sat up, and pulled left into the middle of the road looking for a left-hand turn. The voice said, 'No! Half a mile LEFT!' I turned around and screamed at him, 'WILL YOU FRIGGIN' ARTICULATE!' which prompted the only words I distinctly heard and clearly understood from Ken Gunnels over the entire trip: 'WHY DONT YOU SHOVE IT UP YOUR ASS!' Clear as a bell.

The official finish line was 5.7 miles from the ceremonial finish line at the water's edge. After a short wait at a designated gas station for an official escort vehicle to lead us through the city, all 4 U4H riders joined together for the final parade leg through the empty streets of Annapolis. Loved ones, and in my case, a group of co-workers as well, joined us at the ceremonies at the harbor. Oh, the Joy of it all. . ."

We reach the docks at 4:40 a.m. and ride under a grand, finish line banner into bright lights and cheers. It's dreamlike to see all the smiling faces of friends and family, my cousins and sister. I search for Melinda and there she is, such a beautiful a sight. Tears abound as the fears of the week's ordeal are released; it's over, it's over, it's over, and we are together. All around there are handshakes, hugs and kisses, broad smiles and heartfelt congratulations. I try to introduce Melinda to every one of the gallant crew, and we pose together for dozens of photos, smiles a mile wide that proclaim, *We did it, all of us, together. It's done. We survived the toughest bicycle race in the world.*

Howard Conway

"I drove the late night shift from Parkersburg, WV, to Grafton, WV, my last driving shift. Lewis would drive the rest of the way to Annapolis from there. When we pulled into a gas station around 4:00 in the morning, I was so tired I fell asleep in the driver's seat until the damn phone rang a couple hours later. It was Nate calling to say that Michael and Dave were approximately two hours out. We had to wake everyone and to start duties, food preparation, shower setup, wake the sleeping riders so they could eat and dress. Everyone was so tired at this point that they hated me for waking them. Some people really struggled to wake up. David Eldridge was asleep in the back of his van Karen was asleep in the front. It was just a crappy job, getting them up, but it had to be done. I tried to let some people sleep that did not have to do something right away, like Lewis, as he was preparing for his leg of driving. I climbed in bed in the back with him and we both slept until the riders arrived, then he got up, and I slept on.

Later in the day my wife called my cell phone and I was talking to her lying on the bed, and Lewis was driving so fast, when he hit a bump, I was airborne at least a foot in the air. When you slept in the back, you felt the bump from the front tires and then, a split- second later, you felt the bump in the rear tires and you were often airborne. That's why it was difficult to sleep in the back of the RVs, especially the way we drove.

In Annapolis, we parked the RVs at the hotel and went down to the wharf to see the riders come in. I really needed a shower, but I went down to see the finish anyway. While waiting, worn completely out, I fell asleep on one of the park benches. When I awoke, stiff and sore, I felt homeless. I hated that feeling, and never want to feel that way again. I had survived the RAAM, but I needed and missed the comforts of home. When I was asked if I would every go on a RAAM again, I said I was RAAMR: the R stood for Retired."

The race director in charge of these finish line ceremonies has been sleepless for days, just as we have; he's a hard-working guy. When he introduces us, he prefaces his set-piece accolades with a remark that is as stunning in its inaccuracy as it is for its inappropriateness. *"There has been a protest about United4Health's average age,"* he says, and goes on to mention that a team *intending* to enter the 70+ race *next year* has filed a protest, which is doubly bizarre because if they are not in *this year's race,* they also have no official standing. The race director continues with something to the effect of *"We'll have to wait and see about this new record."*

My teammates and I, our families and supporters are dumbstruck. *What did he say?* We all know our average age is indisputably 70. We know that the RAAM office checks on ages and wouldn't have allowed us into this age category if our average had been lacking. Announcing the charge is also just plain *wrong* in this otherwise celebratory venue, especially since it's an unsubstantiated charge made by an un-credentialed third party, but we are well enough aware of what a week without sleep has done to this poor race director's reasoning, and trust the facts will surface soon enough.

Podium remarks notwithstanding, the facts do eventually surface, and we are officially acknowledged to have averaged 70 years of age. Our official time is 6 days, 13 hours and 13 minutes at an average speed of 19.04 mph, and we do indeed break the existing 70+ record, set in 2004, by 27 hours, as well as besting the 60+ record by more than 3 hours. We incurred no penalties and no serious injuries. We were blessed with shrewd leadership, an outstanding crew, dedicated preparation, fair weather and lots of good luck.

Elena Patterson

"Michael left for California 2 days before the RAAM began, and I was left to my own devices. Those days of anticipation were not fun, so I organized a biking trip on the Eastern Shore of Maryland with the tour company, Bike Vermont. The idea was to have a little cycling holiday distraction with our friends and team supporters while the real race was going on. Our sane and civilized version of the RAAM was a lot of fun even though we were hit by a heat wave, but at least we got to eat and sleep in relaxed and comfortable circumstances. Bike Vermont did a wonderful job, and I am sure they have never had such an unruly group.

I had also decided long before June to put on a celebratory dinner for the team and crew. Aside from planning a location, menu and guest list, I had to commit to a specific date. Was Dave Eldridge's estimate of 168 hours, 7 days exactly, going to be accurate? If so, the team would arrive midday on Saturday, June, 23rd. I took a leap of faith and booked the restaurant for 6 p.m. on that Saturday. What was I thinking? Now the team was under extra pressure to arrive in time for dinner!

Time station progress reports kept reassuring us that they were moving faster than expected. By late Thursday night, an early Saturday morning arrival seemed so certain that we scrambled to book rooms for Friday night, since we had planned to finish our Vermont Bike trip in Annapolis, mid-morning on Saturday. Arriving at the hotel that Friday evening was one of the most exciting days ever. My kids and grandchildren arrived, and Earline joined us for a glass of wine. By then, we knew that the team had done amazingly well, they were all safe, and would be riding in soon. Dave Eldridge called and told us to get some sleep and be down in the lobby at 3:00 a.m. to go down to the docks. I'd had T-shirts made for the families and spectators with the U4H logo. It was pretty great to see this group assembled in the lobby. We all made it out to the docks to wait for the team's arrival and I am sure that morning was one of the most exciting in all of our lives. The team came in looking tired and happy, and it was finally over. After many hard-earned congratulations, they were able to get some sleep back at the hotel and later turned up at the celebration dinner looking a whole lot better.

I would not have been able to keep sane during the race if it had not been for hearing from Lydia and Lewis, but especially Lewis who updated me with comments and photos every few hours. Michael and I had a wedding anniversary during the race, and Lewis sent me a remembrance from Michael as well as constant comments as to how Michael was doing. He also telephoned me every so often, and my cycling group and friends were riveted to these reports. The RAAM was an amazing feat, but if by chance Michael ever thinks of doing it again, my response is going to be: 'Not with this wife '".

Elena's sumptuous celebration dinner is elegant, exhilarating and slightly disorienting in contrast to the rigors of the week. Speeches are made, glasses are raised and the intensity of admiration for what we've accomplished -- as sincere as it is -- is difficult for me to put into perspective. I'm surprised to find myself not quite able to accept the idea that I've done anything special. Ten hours ago, I wanted nothing more than to be done with the RAAM. Now, there's an eerie absence; not because I miss the RAAM's tedium and exhaustion, but because its sudden absence leaves a void that has yet to be filled with anything remotely as engaging. As I glance around the room at the gathering of accomplished, interesting people, it feels as if even a rudimentary level of discourse would be out of reach for me, as if I'll have to re-learn a long-lost language. The reductive simplicity of the week was so single-minded, so self-absorbed, and by necessity, so *infantilizing* that now, with the world suddenly *real* again, the transition back to adult life is sluggishly confusing. For most of a week, all I had to do was pedal; the crew did everything else for me. How often have I gone a day with such attention paid to my every need, let alone a week without a phone, computer, business appointments, family obligations, driving a car, fixing a meal, washing a dish and making the quotidian decisions of everyday life? The RAAM crowded out everything but the racing, and now that it's over, it may take a while for real life to seep back in to the enormous spaces the RAAM commandeered. Here, in the dockside restaurant, I'm experiencing a form Post RAAMatic Stress Disorder.

Michael Scholl

"The victory dinner organized by Elena Patterson in Annapolis was splendid. Michael Patterson recognized every crew member by name and talked about what each person had done to help secure the win. This generous recognition was truly unique as well as touchingly sincere.

After the dinner, even though I was exhausted, I went out to explore the docks with Don, Melinda, Barney and Kayla. Barney and Don had been such a close part of everything I endured for the last 12 days that it was bittersweet knowing this was likely to be the last time that I would see them, but Melinda and Kayla added the perfect counterpoint of grace and beauty to the Spartan rigors of the RAAM," and I counted my week's experience among the best ever."

At the RAAM's racers' banquet the night after Elena's soiree, we learn that the young German Team 26 we met at the starting line in Oceanside, was 2012's fastest 4-person team with a time of 5 days, 18 hours and 55 minutes. They arrived in Annapolis 18 hours and 18 minutes ahead of us (although, if we subtract their average age from our average age, we arrived on earth <u>44 years</u> ahead of *them*.) Among our constant cross-country cohorts, Team Bacchetta was exactly 30 minutes ahead of us. The Spirit of Brazil came in 5 hours and 35 minutes behind us, and the 8-person Georgia Chain Gang was 1 hour and 46 minutes behind us. We also learn that the Forever Young PAC Masters' 80 + team made it across the country in 9 days, 7 hours and 11 minutes at an average of 13.41 mph. What makes their achievement especially remarkable, aside from their *"maturity"*, is that at the beginning of the first day, Lew Stauffer crashed and fractured his hip. For the remaining 2,900 miles, he had to be assisted getting on and off his bicycle, and stood aided by crutches on the podium at Annapolis. Talk about *tough* . . .

The most emotional moment of the evening happens when the 8-man, Wounded Warrior Team 4Mil, comes to the front of the banquet hall to a standing ovation . The applause booms and lasts for several minutes. There's a lump in my throat and tears in my eyes. Eight veterans, with 12 intact legs among them, rode across the country in 7 days, 2 hours and 50 minutes. These are our true champions, our valiant heroes, every one.

I spend the next week mostly off the bike and adopt a blasé insistence that the RAAM was not as stressful as it might have seemed. Partly due to a deep exhaustion that doesn't show in everyday activities, partly due to a, *"What else is there?"* attitude, and partly because I am sick of spending so many hours and so much energy training, I regrettably ignore the needs of a measured recovery. What I *should* be doing is a series of long, easy rides every 2 or 3 days, with lots of rest in between. Instead, I impulsively do a few short, intense rides, and a lot of intense, home improvement carpentry work with no rest at all.

Exactly 2 weeks after completing the RAAM, I enter the Mount Washington hill climb. I've raced this *toughest hill climb in the world* (is there a pattern here?) 6 times, and count it as my favorite, but within the first 2 miles of the 7.6 mile course, I know I'm in trouble. My time at the top is almost 8 minutes slower than my last year's ride. All that training for the RAAM should pay off much better than it is, and presumably would have, if only I'd stuck to a sensible recovery. The effort sets me even deeper into an energy deficit that lasts much of the summer. The RAAM's long term toll on my body was greater than I expected, but much less than it might have been. The big toe on my right foot is permanently numb, but my knee and neck pain have subsided and the vasospasms are gone.

My team mates have better post- RAAM experiences. Although Dur contracts a case of pneumonia in the week after the race, he quickly recovers. Dave continues to ride well all summer with no apparent ill after-effects. Michael also keeps riding extremely well. He and Dur go to Bend, Oregon, for the Masters Nationals in early

September and come home with a gold medal each: Michael in the criterium and Dur in his signature time trial event. If there was ever any question that these guys rode an incredible RAAM, their showings at the Nationals remove all doubt.

Discussions about the RAAM -- especially among non-cyclists -- will always provoke the question: *Why?* But you might as well ask the same question of a guy who's been running three, 8-minute miles a week, and then decides he wants to work his way up to *four,* 8-minute miles a week, or drop his time down to a 7-minute mile pace. What separates him from the RAAM mentality is a difference of *degree*, not a difference of *kind*. Asking *why* is an eternally engaging question, but if you must ask, you're as likely to be bewildered by the answer as the cyclist from whom the answer comes is bewildered by the question.

Melinda Ashley

"When asked 'why put yourself through this?' these athletes' answers are all over the map. My guess is that whatever the answer really is, there's an underlying need for self-validation and praise, knowing that you're better than the next guy and needing that fact to be known. But when the need for that ego-boost goes on perpetually, it seems to be a dead-end, because no amount of race winning and praise will ever be enough. Getting older does not mean getting eternally faster. Praise and recognition for sports achievements may feel good, but they do have a limited shelf life.

I think that self-esteem within the context of aging is by far the most challenging combination facing these older, hyper-competitive athletes. The problem is, whether aging is accepted or not, the process of life goes on, and if non-acceptance is the chosen route, upping the ante for one's physical triumphs is a form of denial, an attempt to delay aging just a little bit longer. The irony is that youthfulness can be extended a lot longer as a state of mind than it can be sustained in a physical body. We can have greater control over our minds that we can over the effects of gravity and oxidization. Remaining youthful lies in our ability to remain flexible and adaptable to life's changes, rather than allowing ourselves to settle into cranky pessimism and loss of enthusiasm. Youthfulness is best measured in our ability to be enthusiastic and connected to others, to remain open-minded, curious and quietly tackle life's everyday problem in ways that are courageous and resourceful, and most of all in our willingness to continue to learn and to grow.

I'm writing this 8 months after the 2012 RAAM. Compared with his mad schedule of training last winter, Don hasn't been on his bike as much or been haunting the gym like he did last year. It's been interesting, how the RAAM has changed his perceptions of competitive racing in general, and of himself in particular. I think writing this book has forced him to examine the nature of competition, the range of motivations that lead to it, and the rewards that follow. Now that it's over (thank God) and the dust has settled, I'm happy to think that the RAAM did him more good than harm. He has definitely mellowed and become easier to be around. He's delighted to have done the RAAM, but he has no desire to do it again, not because it was too difficult, but because, for him, the adventure was in the novelty, and a repeat performance could never be as exciting as the original.

Don also appears to have less interest in a full schedule of competitive events this year, while remaining enthusiastic as ever about cycling with friends. In December, he came back from a wet, muddy cyclocross race (his first, at 72) beaming like a 12-yr old, even though he came in 54th out of 70 racers -- <u>beginners,</u> even! He loves his impromptu bike *rides with his pals Barney, Kayla, Donald and his other beloved "knuckleheads" in NH and VT, and the annual events at Michael and Elena's Old Lyme Bike Camp. And if anyone wants to eat an entire pie at a rest stop or share a 6-pack and a long evening afterwards, he's the first on board without worrying about his training needs. I think this new attitude has nothing to do with fear of aging or laziness, and everything to do with re-discovering his capacity for spontaneous adventure. I'm glad for him, and in this way (only) I'm eternally grateful to the RAAM.*

It's my hope that the courage and strength exemplified by T430's ride across the nation will serve to inspire others to never give up. The accomplishment of this remarkable athletic feat speaks not only about 4 men's tireless devotion to remaining physically fit, but also shows how age itself need not be a limitation to one's readiness to continue to take on new challenges in life, or limit one's ability to overcome obstacles."

"Men do not quit playing because they grow old:
they grow old because they quit playing."

Oliver Wendell Holmes

Coaching

Michael, Dave and Dur's coach, Aidan Charles

"My job is to help cyclists, runners, rowers, and tri-athletes become stronger and faster. My personal roots are in cycling, where I've raced professionally and internationally, and where I've found I was able to reach new levels as an athlete when I had the right tools and coaches at my disposal. Learning how to optimize my training led me to believe that everyone should have access to the same great resources.

My coaching headquarters, CCNS Performance Center in Middletown, CT, is where I do most of my hands-on and face-to-face work with athletes. Much of my work is also via phone conversations and email, which allows me to work with athletes all over the country and beyond. We have a variety of physiological tests and tools to help measure an athlete's physiological profile and limits. With what I do here at the office and how I consult with my athletes, my approach tends to be more scientific and athlete-specific than most. Too often, I find that athletes go out with groups or with an over-generalized training program and they either end up working too little or too hard for consistently beneficial training.

I started working with Michael Patterson in the spring of 2008, and we've worked towards various race goals, year-round, ever since. I've helped him maintain and build his strength through the off-season, manage his training and recovery during the season, and build his specific race strengths for priority events. He has been an awesome athlete to work with because he follows his training plans to a T, and we've become great friends in the process.

The 3 RAAM riders I worked with were in a similar

situation. They all had great race experience, but none of them had done an ultra-endurance event like the RAAM. One key element towards preparing each member for RAAM was getting their bodies ready for the repeated muscular and biomechanical stress they were about to endure. Nothing will stop a rider from riding to their potential like an overuse injury. The race plan was also unique with its alternating 20-min pulls. This type of on-and-off stress puts unique demands on a rider's body (blood pressure changes, digestive tract issues, etc…). We also wanted to increase the actual speed and power that they could put out for the duration of the event. It's one thing to be prepared to survive the RAAM, but it's another thing to prepare to *race* it. We responded to each athlete's personal strengths and limitations, but our overall goals were:

1) Prepare our riders to expend upwards of 3200 kjs per day for 7 days straight.
2) Make sure the riders eat and drink enough while riding and can tolerate digesting food while exercising.
3) Increase the rider's oxidation of fats as fuel, which will help them ride more efficiently and at a higher intensity for long periods of time.

I knew they had the physical capacity to break the record, and I knew they would be fine for the first few days. Everything else depended on how well they stuck to their 20-minute pulls, adequate rest and a proper diet. If they went too hard or didn't eat and drink properly, it would do them in. In retrospect, they pretty much stuck to the plan, and despite a few setbacks, emerged victorious. I was super excited to hear that they broke the record and am proud that I worked with the majority of the team."

Don's coach, Tom Scotto

"I've been working as a professional coach since 2006, when I founded Stage5 Cycling. My approach to coaching is holistic and individualized, addressing biomechanics, metabolic efficiency, nutritional requirements and training, and competition strategy. My interest in cycling includes competition, charity events and cycling in fun and exotic places around the world. I am currently the Director of Education and Sport for Cycling Fusion, which acquired Stage5Cycling in 2010.

I met Don (then age 71) in late November of 2011. He had never been coached during his 15 years of cycling, but now, he wanted to make sure he performed at his best in the 2012 RAAM. Not only was this a monumental ambition in and of itself, he was one of a 4-man team with a focus on breaking the 70+ age record. I've worked with athletes of all ages and have found that each brings a different set of variables to the task, regardless of age. However, masters athletes (35 years old or more) require a greater degree of discipline to train correctly. Masters athletes can ride just as hard as their younger counterparts. They just can't do it as often and must be careful not to over-train and over-fatigue the body.

I pulled Don into my performance lab for VO2 testing and bio mechanic sessions. His conditioning was excellent. I was not surprised because he frequented our weekend group rides and appeared to have no problem keeping up with the "A" group that averaged 18-20 mph. So, based on the testing and on-the-road evidence of Don's fitness, we designed a 7-month program to have him ready by mid-June.

The program was periodized, which allowed us to break the training into smaller blocks in order to make updates to the approach and progression as Don's body adapted.

The first focus was on form and technique, to ensure Don's body was in proper alignment and biomechanics were efficient. This would assist in preventing musculoskeletal fatigue and overuse injuries before the long hours of ultra-endurance training would ensue.

Next, the focus was directed to the specific conditioning Don required both to sustain the long hours in the saddle and to develop the muscular endurance and strength to tackle the many mountain passes.

Don went to AZ for two weeks in the middle of March and to Mallorca for the first two weeks in April, and during each of those trips he rode well over 300 strenuous miles per week, all part of our program design. Every 4th week, he would take it easy, less than 150 miles.

The final 6-week training phase was directed toward race simulation. We were both confident the fitness and endurance had been obtained, however, this one further adaptation was needed to function as part of the 4-man team. This entailed multiple 8-hour training blocks where Don needed to simulate a continuous pattern of riding for 20 minutes and resting for 20 minutes.

Don's determination, discipline and humility during this entire training experience were inspiring. He put his heart and mind into the training, partnered well with his teammates, and succeeded in setting a record that should be on the books for a long, long time."

Dur Higgins

"Before signing on with Michael's RAAM team, I had never been coached in my cycling career of near-ly 30 years. Furthermore, I had used heart monitors and bike computers only briefly, many years ago when they were not reliable, and I had given up on them. And being a "weight-weenie," I didn't think they were worth the weight penalty. My training had always consisted of mostly group rides, and a few solo rides. My only power target was to try to ride the legs off everyone in the peloton over half my age, especially on a mountain climb, of which there are many on Chattanooga rides. I'm sure psychiatrists have a name for such a disorder. I only occasionally rode a trainer, rarely more than 30 minutes or so, and usually between between mirrors to study my TT position. A year after signing on with Michael I was still training 'by the seat of my pants' doing mostly group rides and occasional solo rides. In September 2011, Michael and Elena hosted the team at their Old Lyme, CT home for our first team get-together, and on that visit we met Aidan Charles, Michael's coach for several years. At that time, Michael was the only one of us being coached, or had ever had a cycling coach. Aidan indicated that he wanted to coach the whole team. This idea had great appeal to me: since Michael was depending on me, I should prepare as well as he does, by using his coach. Aidan's commitment to my training would be a commitment to Michael and Dave Burnett as well, as it soon turned out. In the past I had been successful in time trialing, road racing and criteriums, but the RAAM was a very different event, with a much greater emphasis on endurance. I did not know where to start that type of training on my own.

Signing up with Aidan lifted a great burden off me. I no longer had to worry whether I was doing the right training, or enough training; all I had to do was the daily workout he specified and report the data back to him. We began in November, 2011, seven months before RAAM. With my newly acquired Powertap wheel, Garmin computer, heart belt and speed sensors it was easy to measure power, work, cadence vs. time precisely. I soon found that my training was very different from what I would have been doing if left on my own. Initially, I was assigned long endurance rides of much greater duration and frequency than I had ever done in winter. At first, I tried to keep riding with friends, but I soon found I could not do the assigned workouts on group rides. I also found I could do the long rides, at specified power levels, much better inside on my trainer! I was home with Earline more, I wasn't driving so much going to and from rides, often on the other side of town, and I was lessening my chances of a bike wreck that might take me out before the race. Watching a power meter and following a workout spec helps pass the time, but watching TV with headphones really helps. One of my favorite things to watch was a DVD "Team 409, Oceanside to Annapolis" about the 4-man Hoosier team that broke the 60+ RAAM record in 2010. This was a valuable reference for learning about the RAAM, but also it served to make me realize that we might also be able to break the 60+ record. I am sure I watched the Team 409 movie 50 times during my many long workouts. At one point, I was doing three workouts per week of 6 hours each, plus about 4 hours worth of shorter rides! 22 hours/week in the saddle! As we transitioned from winter to spring, the workouts went from long and steady to shorter but more intense with lots of power intervals. Also, we began doing 'Race Simulation' training in the last months before the race. Most of my Race-Sim workouts I did from the shaded parking lot of a church, located on a 7-mile loop with almost no traffic. The folks on that loop must have thought me crazy. A couple of them did stop to check me out, thinking I was cycling's answer to Forest Gump.

My first tries at Race-Sim were a shock. I had never had to go through such a workout in all of my career. The holy grail of athletics is to warm up thoroughly before going hard. But starting cold and pushing hard caused great pain and discomfort in my quadriceps. I tried using Hammer Nutrition Race Caps Supreme and found it helped a lot, apparently buffering the lactic acid buildup. I finally decided that for the race I would take one RCS capsule per hour, or one per bottle of water. My last week of long workouts was 5/6/2012, leaving 5 weeks of taper before RAAM. During that week, my training schedule was:

Sun: 5 hour ride at aerobic stim=95 mi ("stim" = pace)

Mon: 5 hr ride at aerobic stim with one 15 min interval=100 mi

Tues: 1 hr easy spin on trainer

Wed: 6 hrs of race sim=63 mi (20 mins. on, 20 mins. off)

Thu: 4 hr ride at aerobic stim=80 mi

Fri: 1 hr spin on trainer

Sat: 6 hours race sim=63 mi. Total for the week = 27 hours, 400 + miles"

Team Bike Specs

Each of us brought two bikes to the RAAM. We also had with us a spare set of wheels, adaptable to either bike, and a bag full of *what-if* spare parts, extra shoes, cleats, pedals, derailleurs and chains. Although we are all veteran cyclists with a healthy collection of bikes among us, the prospect of a 3,000-mile Odyssey prompted the sirens of *BestBikeInTheWorld* to begin their seductive song. Since we could easily argue that the RAAM would be the apogee of our careers, we considered brands, models and components we'd previously thought prohibitively exotic. We developed and discarded multiple theories of what the RAAM would require of our equipment, and spent hours comparing the weights, aerodynamics and durability of esoteric components. Some of us derisively dismissed the "WeightWeenies" website -- which provides, gram-by-gram comparisons of even the most infinitesimal components -- even as we consulted it in search of perfection. There was talk about testing our bikes, our clothing and riding positions in a wind tunnel, but nothing came of this beyond the feeling that we were *intending* to be hyper-diligent. All of this pre-race preoccupation was a welcome distraction from our increasingly demanding training schedule and even, possibly, occasionally, probably *useful*.

One of our two bikes was a racing bike, a variety most recognizable to most people. It is lightweight, relatively comfortable and equipped with gear ratios suitable for fast flats as well as steep climbs. It handles well, and although it is not designed to be optimally aerodynamic, it can be ridden all day in a wide range of conditions. This bike was the easier of the two to select, and because it was the most familiar and least subject to extreme modification, we seemed to make our choices early on, some of which were to simply use the road bike we already owned.

The TT bike decision was more complicated. Dur and Michael had experience owning and racing TTs, but Dave and I had never touched one. The TT's pros and cons are thoroughly covered in previous chapters, so I won't repeat them here, but overall, we were as well equipped as anyone in the RAAM could be. When the huge variety of terrain, road surfaces and bio-mechanical responses to fatigue are factored in, it's possible that our record-setting performance could have been achieved with a less exotic stable of mounts, but that theory shall be forever speculative. For readers interested in gear, the bikes were as follows:

Road Bikes

Dave Burnett: Trek Madone, Shimano Dura-Ace drive train with 50-34 gearing at the crank and an 11-23, 10-spd. rear cassette. ZIPP 404 carbon wheels with Continental Sprinter, 700x23 tubular tires.

Dur Higgins: Scott Addict R1. SRAM Red gruppo, 50-34 and 11-28, 10-spd. gear sets. Bontrager 3D3 carbon wheels with Continental Sprinter, 700x22 tubular tires.

Don Metz: Scott Addict R1. SRAM Red gruppo, 50-34 and 11-28, 10-spd. gear sets. Reynolds 400 carbon wheels with Michelin Pro 3 Race, 700x23 clincher tires.

Michael Patterson: Serotta Meivici. Shimano Dura-Ace with DI2 electronic shifters, 50/34 and 11/28, 10-spd. gear sets. Bontrager XXX super-light carbon wheels with Vittoria Open Corsa Evo CX, 700x23 clincher tires.

Time Trial Bikes

Dave Burnett: Trek Speed Concept. Shimano Dura-Ace with D12 electronic shifters. 53-39 and 11-23 10-spd gear sets. Bontrager 909 wheels, 282 mm front, 292 mm rear with Vittoria Open Corso Evo 700x23 clinchers and latex tubes.

Dur Higgins: 2006 Cervelo P3C , Shimano Dura-Ace 53-39 and 11-23, 10-spd gear sets. Zipp 808 Firecrest (2012 model) rear wheel with Continental Sprinter, 700x22 tubular tire; Zipp 808, (2006 model) front wheel with Continental Competition, 700x19 tubular tire.

Don Metz: 2010 Parlee TT, SRAM Red gruppo, 53-39 and 11-28, 10-spd. gear sets. Reynolds SVD66T carbon rear wheel, Reynolds DV46ULT carbon front wheel, both wheels with Vittoria Open Corsa Evo CX, 700x23 clinchers and latex tubes.

Michael Patterson: Trek Speed Concept TT. Shimano Dura-Ace with DI2 electronic shifters, 53-39 and 11-25, 10-spd. gear sets. Zipp 404 wheels with Vittoria Open Corsa Evo CX 700x23 clinchers and latex tubes.

Racer Biographies

David Burnett (68) Norwich, CT
Dave has competed in just about any manner available to him since grammar school. Football was his primary interest through high school, but a senior year knee injury kept him from success at the collegiate level. With that void in his life he bought a motorcycle, began racing motocross, had some success, flunked out of college and moved to California to race. While there and while enjoying racing, he began to reclaim his academic standing, eventually completing his undergraduate work at San Diego State University. After having a great time racing, family and career became his primary focus. He and his wife, Nancy, have 3 children who continue to impress and fascinate them. Vocationally, he runs a mental health center which he has directed since he was the only employee in 1978. Today he has 265 employees, and he loves his work. In his 40's and 50's, running became an interest, then a passion, and he enjoyed some success in local races. At the age of 59, his old football knee injury caught up with him, and he began biking to rehab the knee. This quickly led to an interest in racing bikes. His racing resulted in a podium finish in the 2008 USCF Masters Nationals and several years as the Masters Cycle Racing Association Champion (age 60 plus) of the northeast district of the USCF. The RAAM was an exciting culmination of a life of happy competition.

Durward Higgins (70) Chattanooga, TN
Born in El Paso, TX, Dur earned his BS in Mechanical Engineering in 1966 from Texas Western College. He had a 32-year career with General Electric in a variety of Tur-

bine Field Engineering capacities. He retired at 56 and has been married to Earline since 1983. They have 5 children (his 2, her 3) and 7 grandchildren.

Dur was born loving anything with wheels and grew up with a car-enthusiast father who had an auto repair/service business, where Dur worked from age 14 to 21. During college he was a bodybuilder and reached 204 muscular lbs. At 23, he learned he had high blood pressure -- too high to pass the draft physical. In his 30s, he played tennis, trying his best to get good at it, but soon decided he was not a natural athlete.

At age 38, he learned he had high cholesterol, as well as high blood pressure, and began running on doctor's orders. Coincidently, he was told he had an unusually high VO2 max and eventually realized that was why he was endowed with an above-average bicycle engine. He began racing at age 40, with the Tennessee State Road Championships his annual goal, especially time trialing. After he turned 60, he won three 60+ Best All-Around Rider jerseys, and 10 time-trial, road and crit state championships. At 65, he returned to the Masters National Championships for the first time since age 45, and has been back 4 years, medaling 6 times, including a National Championship in the Time-Trial 2009 and silver in the Criterium 2008. In 2008-2010, he raced the Huntsman World Senior Games and won 9 medals, including 2 golds, 3 silvers, and 4 Bronzes. At the National Senior Olympics in San Francisco, 2009, he won 3 golds and a bronze in the 4 road cycling events. He also won the Best Overall 65+ Rider awards at both the Nationals and Huntsman Games in 2009. After RAAM, Dur won another TT National Championship, and gold at the Huntsman World Senior Games in the Hillclimb TT.

Don Metz (72) Lyme, NH; Arlington, MA

When he's not on his bike, Don is an award-winning residential architect and author. His attraction to speed began at age 13, racing jalopies around a hayfield on the family farm in Pennsylvania. The excitement of competition led to track teams in high school and at Yale, where he was a member of two IC4A championship teams. Running the 880 gave way to motorcycle racing in the early 70's, and wilderness adventures in the 80's. The mountain biking bug bit in the mid-90's, and for three seasons, Don was a silver and gold medalist at the Huntsman Senior Games in St. George, Utah. His first (and only) road race resulted in a bronze at the 2007 National Seniors' Games 20k in Louisville, KY. Since 2008, Don has regularly climbed the podium at the 9-event New England Hill Climb series (BUMPS), and at age 69, he set a 65-69 age group record on Mt. Washington. Don has 3 remarkable children and 2 granddaughters he spoils whenever possible. When he's not designing houses or writing books, he builds more-or-less legal mtn. bike trails all over his hometown of Lyme, NH where he lives with his wife Melinda and Marley the cat.

Michael Patterson (70) New York, NY; Old Lyme, CT

Michael started biking in his early 40's, after 30 years of ice hockey through school, Harvard and beyond had taken their toll on his knees and back. His passion for cycling grew over twenty years, edging other sports aside, and he eventually tried his first race at age 63, just to see if he was really any good. He was, and was instantly hooked. Now retired from two careers, first as a law partner at Debevoise &Plimpton, then as a vice chairman of JPMorgan Chase, Michael is a committed bike racer, competing around the country in time trials, road races and criteriums (in which discipline he won the 2012 national 70+ championship). He spends his free time on board work for land conservation, education for special needs children, bio-ethics, and USA Cycling (the national governing body for competitive cycling). Michael and his wife, Elena, also an avid and competitive cyclist, have three children and six amazing, sports-crazed grandkids.

Crew Biographies

Dave Eldridge

Dave has been a crew leader for RAAM five times, supporting Team Type 1 as they finished first in the eight-man division of RAAM from 2006-2010, and set an eight-man RAAM record in 2009. In 2012, he brought his winning style of leadership to the United4Health team and its 70+ record.

Karen Scheerer

Having played the roles of nutritionist, photographer, logistics coordinator, cheerleader and "team mom," Karen brought a variety of those experiences to her third year in the RAAM. Karen lives in Nashport, Ohio, where she gardens, takes photographs and spoils her grandchildren.

Michael Scholl

Michael's first crew experience for a RAAM team was in 2007, when he served as photographer and provided logistical support. Since then, he has kept a RAAM blog to help share with readers the pain and elation that these athletes experience as they push themselves day and night for 3,000 miles.

Barney Brannen

First-time RAAM volunteer, Barney Brannen, a lawyer, lives in Thetford, VT, and is an avid cyclist, skier, and hockey player. Barney and Michael Scholl drove and navigated the racer RV at speeds considered just right by their passengers, while judged to be much too slow by the lead-footed drivers of the crew's RV.

Lydia Brewster

In addition to being a social worker who manages a Connecticut soup kitchen, Lydia brings 35 years of experience in massage to the team. Her constant attention to the overworked bodies of the racers was a crucial component of the team's success. The RAAM was her first and, she politely insists, her last.

Janice Smolowitz

As an RN, nurse practitioner and teacher, Jan took a leap of faith and signed on to the RAAM with no prior experience in endurance cycling or its odd customs. Undaunted, she quickly established herself as a key player among the crew where her good will and medical skills were invaluable.

212

Ken Gunnells

Ken teaches Information Systems in the School of Business at the University of Alabama in Birmingham. He's an avid recreational cyclist and student of GPS programming, navigation and logistics. Ken shared driving and navigating the follow van with Greg and John. 2012 was his third RAAM.

Chris Champion

Chris, from Hershey, PA, shared the navigator/driver duties in the racer van with Taylor Keaton and Nate Keck. When he's not riding one of his bikes or piloting a Cessna, Chris teaches Computer Information Systems at a vocational-technical school. The 2012 event was his second RAAM experience.

Taylor Keaton

Taylor is a professional mechanic who lives in Chattanooga, Tennessee with the love of his life and their amazing dog. Taylor, Nate and Chris were the drivers and navigators of the racer van. A RAAM rookie, Taylor jumped at the chance to help keep the team's racers and bikes running smoothly.

Greg Thompson

For his first RAAM, Greg joined the United4Health crew as a follow van driver/navigator and mechanic. For 9 years, he's helped keep bikes running in the "RAG-BRAI", the annual cycling pilgrimage across Iowa. Greg is a trials rider and downhill biking enthusiast with over 10 years of experience as a bike mechanic.

Howard Conway

Howard has always been on an adventure, from high school and college athletics to coaching at the youth and high school levels. 2012 was his first RAAM experience. He was co-driver and navigator of the speedy crew RV with Lewis Runnion. Howard was eager to add RAAM to his list of excursions, affectionately called "Conway Adventures" by his children and grandchildren.

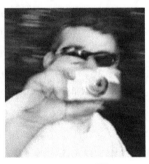

Manny Casillas

A true outdoorsman, Manny lives in Austin, Texas, where you'll find him camping, kayaking, cycling, running, adventure racing or working at REI as an REI Outdoors School Instructor. He has many marathons and ultra-marathons under his belt, and has crewed for dozens of long distance cycling events.

John Markley

John lives in Tucson, AZ, where he enjoys cycling and doing woodworking projects while attempting to figure out "Career 3.0." His personal goals in the 2012 RAAM (his first) were to assist wherever/whenever possible, stay awake, and not smell too bad, all but one of which he accomplished with distinction.

Nate Keck

Nate has been a RAAM crew member/coach for three previous races, including the record-setting, eight-man team Type 1. He's been the head cycling coach for Colorado Mesa University, and is currently at Marian University in Indianapolis, where he coaches the top collegiate cycling team in the USA.

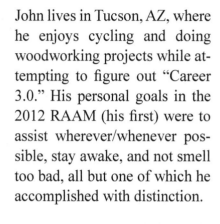

Lewis Runnion

Lewis is the Director of Military Affairs for Bank of America Merrill Lynch, and a former military officer. 2012 was his first RAAM. Lewis and Howard were the notorious drivers and navigators of the speedy crew RV. Lewis is an avid cyclist and serves on the boards of a number of charitable organizations.

Acknowledgements

Our Race Across America at 19.04 mph happened so fast that I wondered how I could ever re-capture it on the page, but as I accustomed myself to the keyboard's limit of .004 mph, the particulars came back into focus. Fortunately, my recollections were further enhanced by the memories and perspectives of a dozen collaborators whose written testimonies give a nuanced breadth and depth to the narrative. Thanks to all of you who captured your memories so well, and to those whose generous conversations added to my ability to re-construct the journey. To my preposterously fast teammates, Dave, Dur and Michael, I salute you ! You will always be an inspiration to me -- and to all those unfortunates who presume to ride as fast and long as you three do, I wish the best of luck. *Didn't we have a blast ?!*

I'm immensely grateful to our unflappable crew chief Dave Eldridge, and to every one of our gallant crew members for their tolerance, skills and sacrifices. I promise I will never again intentionally deprive anyone of a week's worth of palatable food or a reasonable night's rest. To the husbands, wives and sweethearts of the crew and racers, thanks for your infinite patience during what must have at times seemed like an eternity of waiting for that final pedal stroke.

To Harvey "Not-a-Geek" Brotman, I owe many gigabytes of thanks for his patience ushering this stubborn Luddite through the mysterious maze of a digital domain that even my granddaughters find obvious. To Barney Brannen, steadfast friend, sacrificial crew member and astute counselor/writer/editor, my gratitude is infinite. Neil Goodwin's advice on writing and life, always astute and true, was just right, as always. I'm also deeply indebted to Karen Scheerer, indispensible RAAM *uber* Mom and team photographer, for her beautiful design of the book's covers, despite my constant meddling. For my wife Melinda, whose adaptation to the foreign world of the RAAM's die-hard culture was never easy, I hold both a profound respect and an enormous gratitude. Her shrewd and unshakeable insights, steadfast support and brave forbearance have pulled me through many a tough patch. She is my rock.

If it weren't for Michael and Elena Patterson, our memorable race would have never happened. The Pattersons paved every inch of the way with modesty, grace and wisdom. Their contributions to the cycling community, near and far, has been, and will continue to be, an immeasurable gift to the sport. From everyone connected to the 2012 United-4Health RAAM adventure, *Thank You Michael and Elena!*

About The Author

Don Metz is a practicing residential architect specializing in energy-efficient design. He is an award-winning pioneer in the development of earth-sheltered homes and continues to design exceptional houses throughout New England. His work has appeared in publications ranging from the *New York Times* to *Architectural Record*. He is the author of five books on various aspects of construction and architecture, and two novels, *Catamount Bridge*, and *King of the Mountain,* published by HarperCollins. Cycling has been an important part of his life since the 1990s, when he traded his running shoes and sore knees for a mountain bike and scraped knees. He is lately adamant about not writing or practicing architecture on warm, sunny days when he could be out in the woods or on a bike. It wasn't until quite a few months after the RAAM that the notion of writing a book about it held him chair-bound over the winter of 2012-2013.

CPSIA information can be obtained
at www.ICGtesting.com
Printed in the USA
BVHW040316121219
566449BV00011B/141/P